FROM THE TOP DOWN

FROM THE TOP DOWN
THE NUTS AND BOLTS OF LAUNCHING AND LEADING A CHURCH

Michael Lukaszewski, Jr.

Copyright © 2010 by Michael Lukaszewski, Jr.

All rights reserved. No part of this book may be reproduced, stored, or transmitted by any means—whether auditory, graphic, mechanical, or electronic—without written permission of both publisher and author, except in the case of brief excerpts used in critical articles and reviews. Unauthorized reproduction of any part of this work is illegal and is punishable by law.

Hardcover ISBN: 978-0-557-50199-1

Paperback ISBN: 978-0-557-50198-4

CONTENTS

Every Church Begins With a Story		1
Chapter 1:	Shut Down the Engine and Put Up the Sails	5
Chapter 2:	A Blog, A Conference, and a Coaching Network	17
Chapter 3:	Other Crazy People	31
Chapter 4:	Big Vision Takes Big Money (Or Does It?)	41
Chapter 5:	The Pipes In the Wall	53
Chapter 6:	Bullhorns and Postcards	67
Chapter 7:	What We Want to Do Well, Part One	81
Chapter 8:	What We Want To Do Well, Part Two	93
Chapter 9:	It Feels Like It Takes a Village	103
Chapter 10:	Groups and Classes	113
Chapter 11:	On Being Portable	121
Chapter 12:	Getting the Right People On the Bus	129

Chapter 13:	Parting Shot	139
Appendix 1:	52 Offering Talk Ideas	141
Appendix 2:	What's included on the Docs and Forms CD	145

EVERY CHURCH BEGINS WITH A STORY

If every church begins with a story, chapter one of the Oak Leaf story is titled *Reluctance*.

After a dozen years in student ministry, my wife and I believed God was calling us to Atlanta to start a new church – even though there were tons of churches there and we didn't know a single person.

I wasn't sold on Cartersville because, even though the town of 20,000 had a Wal-Mart, it didn't have much else. There was no mall. There were no sports teams. The movie theater was a dingy, eight-screen complex that would scare roaches away. Cartersville did have an extraordinary number of banks, Waffle Houses and cows. Those seemed to be the selling points.

Having grown up in a large city, small-town America wasn't for me. I didn't own a gun, and I don't watch NASCAR. But since we sold our house and were committed to the general area of Atlanta, we rented an apartment in Cartersville and moved forward. My plan was to use Cartersville as a home base to find the *real* place where we could launch a church. I woke up every morning, and set out in any given direction looking for the perfect place. After about 150 miles on the odometer, I'd come back home.

Not only did I feel like a fish out of water in this small town, I didn't feel qualified to be a "real pastor". Having been a youth pastor for a dozen years, I knew about teenagers, but I didn't know about starting churches. And the more books I read and models I investigated, the more confused I became. I felt like I was an 18-year-old youth pastor all over again.

During the next few months, God went to work on my heart. On Sundays, we would drive forty-five minutes to attend West Ridge Church, and during the week, I would drive around looking for potential sites. We met a few real-life families, and when we realized that this place wasn't just a town, but that it was full of people who didn't really go to church, something changed.

It helped that we heard they would be building a Starbucks. And I figured I could buy a gun and put a Number 8 sticker on my Jeep.

In October of 2005, I had an information meeting in a hotel meeting room. Six families attended that first meeting. I talked about the vision for a new church, a church that would be grounded on truth but relevant to the culture. A church where people could come as they are, without having to put on their best clothes or smiles.

In January of 2006, we started meeting as a launch team. We met on Sunday nights and talked through core values and church philosophies. Sometimes, we would attend a church plant on Sunday morning and talk about our experiences that evening. As the months went on, we began dividing up responsibilities. *Julie, you're our head greeter. Melissa, you work with preschoolers.* We had no worship leader and no place to meet. And neither of those things seemed to be on the horizon.

Over the next few months, our launch team grew to about twelve families. Every school I talked to denied me. Any room in Cartersville that was large enough to hold one hundred people either wasn't available or wasn't going to be rented to a church. There was only one possibility, and construction on that place wasn't even finished.

In May of 2006, I was attending the Buzz Conference in Washington, D.C. Part of that conference was a breakout on doing church in a movie theater. While attending that breakout, Tim (our other staff member) got word that we would definitely be able to use the brand new Carmike movie theater. They had torn down the old theater, and built the first all-digital theater in the state of Georgia. This was good news, since we had a preview service scheduled in a few weeks!

Our launch team was fired up, and the responsibilities were all divided up. We scraped together all the money we had and bought some road signs and designed a postcard. I know a lot of church plants that do multiple massive mailouts, but we just had enough money to send out five thousand postcards.

The first preview service was in June of 2006, and 140 people showed up. We did another one a month later, and there were 180 people. In August of 2006, we held our grand opening service and there were 250 people in attendance.

Oak Leaf Church was born. Thirteen months into it, there were nine hundred people crammed into three services. And we're still not really sure how it all happened.

CHAPTER 1:
SHUT DOWN THE ENGINE AND PUT UP THE SAILS

M oses was called by God to lead God's people out of slavery into the Promised Land. David was called by God to take out a nine-footer with a slingshot. The first disciples were asked to leave their nets to follow Jesus.

And I was called by God to start a church.

But the call of God on my life looks a little different than the burning bush saga. In fact, I'm convinced that just as God created people differently, he calls people uniquely.

My call into church planting wasn't instant; it was gradual. I didn't read a verse that made it all make sense. I didn't have a dream or hear a voice or see a billboard. Instead, God worked in my heart over a couple of years.

Toward the end of my youth ministry years, I found myself dreaming of what a different kind of church would be like. I found myself wanting to attend leadership conferences that weren't created for youth pastors. For years, I'd attended conferences like The National Youth Workers Convention, put on by Youth Specialties. But conferences like the Creative Church Conference seemed more appealing to me for some reason.

I noticed that I wasn't buying youth ministry books anymore. Instead, I was reading books about church in general. More and more of my conversations drifted into discussions about discipleship, or families, or programming.

Think of the church like a ship that has different parts. You've got the port side and the stern side (why can't they just call them left and right?). You've got the galley and the crew's quarters. Different people are in charge of different parts of the ship. But no matter how well the cook runs the kitchen, the whole boat is going in one direction. I realized that no matter how well my individual ministry was operating, if the entire ship wasn't going in the right direction we wouldn't find success.

I guess I just started caring more about where the boat was going.

I haven't given up on student ministry, and I still believe that working with students is one of the highest callings in life. But a great Wednesday night youth service is not the hope of the church. There are churches all across the world that have strong youth programs, and the students that leave those strong youth programs when they graduate, leave the church. Part of the problem is that while we work hard to make sure teenagers have good programming; we don't work hard to integrate them into the whole church. I believe that they leave the church because they were never a part of the church in the first place.

As a youth pastor, I saw hundreds of kids committed to their youth group, but not to their church. Worse yet, I saw hundreds of teenagers committed to their youth group, but not God. I accept the responsibility of this, but as I realized this I decided that the American church needed to do something.

There are churches with strong worship teams, but the church isn't seeing much impact. There are churches that care about missions, but things aren't functioning on all cylinders. There are churches that have great teachers but still struggle to impact their community. One part of the ship working right doesn't mean the boat is headed in the right direction.

It was time for me to steer the ship. But I was scared to take the wheel.

EXCUSE TIME

When God called Abraham in Genesis 12, He promised to bless him, make him famous, bless those who were nice to him, curse those who were mean to him, and bless everybody on the planet through Him. Talk about pressure.

But none of this would happen until Abraham obeyed, packed up his stuff, left Haran, and headed in the general direction of Canaan.

How would you have responded if you were Abraham?

- But God, I'm seventy-five years old. I'm way too old for this cross-country trek.
- But God, my wife is sixty. She's not the spring chicken that she once was.
- But God, all my friends and family are here.
- But God, you're not even telling me where I'm going. That's just not good planning.

I'm impressed that Abraham got started on his journey the very next day. He packed up all his stuff and got going. He didn't take 40 days to pray about it. He didn't ask his small group what they thought God wanted. He didn't ride his camel down to the local Christian book tent to look for answers. He just obeyed. That wasn't my response when God told me to go start a church. I'm sad to say that I made some excuses.

- I didn't think I was old enough. I was thirty-one years old, married, and the father of one little girl. But I thought it would be better if I was a few years older before beginning this journey.
- I didn't have enough money in the bank. Actually, I didn't have any money in the bank. I knew that starting a church wasn't a real stable job, and that it would probably take some start up money, and those were things that I thought would come later.
- I had passion, but I really didn't know enough. What did I know about starting a church? It's one thing to get high school students to listen to me talk, but we're taking about adults. Teaching adults is scary.

I wonder what all these excuses sounded like to God. Here's the God of the universe, the giver of breath, the maker of all things, and

I'm telling him that I'm not old enough! Here's the one who owns everything there is and will ever be, a God with limitless resources, and I'm telling him that I don't have enough money.

In the middle of making excuses, someone called me with a job offer. A *good* job offer. An offer to be the high school pastor at a prominent megachurch. Though I knew deep down that God wanted me to go start a church, I accepted the job.

One month into the job, I felt like Jonah, the Old Testament prophet who went left when God told him to go right. I had run from the call of God. I had pursued my own comforts over the call of God. Looking back on it, I wish I was more like Abraham and less like Jonah. I wish I had obeyed the next day instead of running away.

See, it's one thing to know what God is telling you to do, but it's another thing to do it. I'm convinced that a lot of Christians know what God wants them to do. We try and make "finding God's will" into some kind of secret pursuit, as if God is hiding his will and trying to make it difficult for us to discover. I think the hardest part of being a Christian is not finding God's will, it's *doing* it.

We muddy up the call of God with our reasons, excuses, and way of living. We believe following God is too hard or too costly, so we just pretend like we don't know what to do. We ask people to pray for our financial situation even though we know we'd be well on to the solution if we didn't lease that car. We ask people to pray for our kids, when we know that God wants us to spend more time with them. We want God to show us the way, but we don't want to get up that early to go to church.

Another thing that we Christians do is focus on all the confusing stuff, when the simple stuff is right there before our eyes. Some Christians want to get together to talk about what predestination really means. Some want to argue about dispensationalism or discuss the finer points of theology. I'm convinced that being a Christian is more about following Jesus—loving God and loving your neighbor. I'm pretty sure that Jesus knew exactly what he was saying when he said those were the greatest commandments.

There's an insane number of blogs devoted to the "deep stuff." All the while, we let the simple but profound command of Jesus to love our neighbor fall by the wayside. If we're not careful, all the carefully worded arguments can become carefully placed excuses.

Like Jonah, I ran away from the call of God because I let the excuses become reasons. When I did that, I was putting more faith in myself than in God. And just a few months into the megachurch job, I knew that I was running from God and decided that it was time to run back.

The detour lasted about nine months, and God orchestrated the circumstances in such a way that we had a second chance. This time, there would be no running. Jonah reluctantly gave into God's call and went to Nineveh. He preached a half-hearted sermon and went to wait for God to judge the people that he'd preached to in Nineveh. Jonah was ticked when the people actually listened to his message and repented. He was mad that God didn't destroy them, and in the final chapter of the book, God taught him a lesson. We never find out if Jonah came to grips with it all or if he died a reluctant prophet.

We sold our house, the one we had owned for a total of six months, and moved to Georgia. We were headed to the place where God wanted us to go in the first place, about one year late.

I think there's only one good reason to start a church, but before I go there, I want to talk about a few of the bad ones.

BAD REASONS TO START A CHURCH

1. **You want to be your own boss.** Too many people rush into church planting because they can't thrive in another ministry position. They can't be under authority, so they just want to become the authority. They don't like taking orders, so they decide they will give them. A florist might get tired of answering to a boss, so she opens her own flower shop. But it doesn't work like that in church planting.
2. **You hate your current church.** Having worked in different churches for a dozen years, I saw lots of things wrong with the modern church. I saw a lot of things that I wished were different. Out-of-date programs needed to go. The simple message of Jesus needed to come to the forefront. The politics needed to go out the window. But a knee-jerk reaction to all that's wrong with the church will not help you establish a healthy new one. If we're not careful, we're going to start a

bunch of churches based on what's wrong with our previous churches. There are too many ticked off youth pastors who think they can teach better than the real pastor, so they saddle up to plant a church.
3. **You just want to teach.** I do believe that communicating is one of the most important things a church planter does. In fact, I think most church planters don't develop this gift enough. But there's more to church planting than just teaching and preaching. If you just want to teach, write one good message, and then hit the circuit. Teaching is a critical component, but it's not the only one. There are guys that want to be rock-star communicators and figure starting a church is a sure-fire way to get an audience.

ONE REALLY BAD REASON

I slept through most of Art History in college and have a hard time telling the difference between a Rembrandt and a Picasso. I think one of those guys cut off his ear and the other one was crazy.

Realism became popular in the mid-nineteenth century, as a push back to the romantic ideals and imagination of Romanticism. Then you've got Impressionism, which is a style of painting. Those artists apply paint in small touches rather than in broad strokes, to try and capture a scene as if you just had a glimpse of it. Impressionism is the watercolor looking art, the kind of thing that looks like children produced it.

Throughout history, art has reacted to the period before it. Realism gives way to Romanticism because society gets worn out on what looks real. Impressionism gives way to Romanticism because, well, I think because people got tired of sappy paintings. It's not just true in the art world either.

Skinny ties of the 1980s followed fat ties of the 1970s. Counting fat grams turns into counting carbohydrates. Democrats vote out the Republicans. Sunday school becomes small groups. Modern becomes postmodern which becomes emergent. Nobody really knows what emergent will become because nobody can really define it now.

Every movement pushed back on the movement right before.

Yahoo Groups currently lists 140 different denominations including Baptist, Seventh Day Baptist, Virtual Church, United Church of Christ, United Church of God, Congregational Christian, Armenian Evangelical and Free Presbyterian. Denominations can be a good thing, but this is getting a little ridiculous.

There are more than twenty-six hundred groups that claim to be the true church. Most of these denominations were formed because of something someone didn't agree with in a previous denomination. We're always reacting to something that happened right before us, and this is one of the biggest dangers in church planting.

Instead of launching a church because God calls us, we launch a church as a reaction to the way we were brought up. We want to start a relevant church because we were in a traditional church. We want to use the NLT because we were forced to use the KJV. We want to be missional because we used to be attractional. Instead of starting a church out of a deep passion for shaping the future, we start churches out of a deep hatred of something in our past.

An effective church cannot be built on new methodologies or new trends. The flavor of the month won't create a healthy church. A new book or the latest, greatest conference can't be your foundation.

All of these things change from time to time; they provide valuable insights, but you can't build a church on these things. A new church can't simply be a reaction.

ONLY ONE GOOD REASON

There's only one good reason that you should plant a church. And it's really quite simple. You should only plant a church because God has called you to plant a church. If you think you'd like to do something else in life or in ministry, go do it! If you think anything else would make you happier, then pursue that! My first advice to people thinking about planting churches is to make sure that's what God wants. It can't be a good idea—it has to be a God idea.

Bill Hybels talks about having a holy discontent, that thing that keeps you up at night and requires your action. When you look at the world not just with a distaste of the current movement or trend, but also with eyes of compassion. A deep desire.

That is the call of God. And if that call is not burning inside of you, compelling you to do something, then you *must* find something else to do.

In 1517, an Augustinian Monk and a professor at the University of Wittenberg started a protest about the sale of indulgences. Tradition tells us that the church was selling these indulgences, the release from the temporary penalties of sin in order to raise money to build St. Peter's in Rome. Martin Luther nailed his 95 Theses onto the door of the church, and with the help of the printing press, a revolution began.

Luther was burdened with the fact that the Bible taught justification by faith, while the church seemed to teach justification by works. The Catholic Church responded with the Council of Trent, but the separation was underway. Luther's passion, his holy discontent, drove him and set the protestant reformation in motion. He saw a problem and was compelled to do something. It wasn't just a reaction to the sale of indulgences; it was a deep-rooted passion that God wanted to do something. It was his holy discontent. His clear call from God.

JR Lee[1], a church planter in the Atlanta area says this:

> Planting a church because it's cool? - Buy a new car. Because it is exciting? - Buy a skydiving session and go jump out of an airplane. Because you hate the one you're in? - Find a new one and invest your life there. Because you want to be the "lead" pastor? - Check your motives and make sure there is more to it than that. We need more churches and we need more church planters. Just make sure that it wasn't your idea. Make sure you were called to do this thing. Any other reason and you WILL fail. That's what will sustain you. Answer the call—just make sure that is what you are answering.

My friend Tadd[2], a church planter in North Carolina says it this way:

> My fear is that church planting has become what youth ministry was 10 years ago. Everyone coming out of

---

[1] jrlive.net
[2] taddgrandstaff.com

college wanted to be a youth pastor back then. Now, everyone coming out of college wants to jump straight into church planting. Most of these guys have never had a full-time ministry position in their life. Most of these guys have never had to deal with any type of church issues. Most of these guys are in such an incredible hurry to run off and start a church that they aren't willing to slow down, learn the ropes, and understand what they are about to get into. They just see "cool" churches, playing "cool" music, and wearing "cool" clothes, and they say, "Sign me up."

Both of these guys are saying that there's more to church planting than wanting to reach people, or wanting to do church in a new way. They are both saying that the call of God is the most important factor.

IT'S A SAILBOAT, NOT A MOTORBOAT

I like to listen to sermons while I run on a treadmill. I love Mark Driscoll but I can't listen to him on the treadmill because I don't want to run for ninety-three minutes. One morning, I was listening to John Piper, and he gave one of the greatest illustrations I've ever heard in my life. I literally got off the treadmill and went back to my house so I could write it down.

Piper said that it's too easy to turn the church into a motorboat, when she's really a sailboat.

We can work hard and manufacture the whole thing if we want. We can put gas in the engine, fire that thing up and make some waves. It's an amazing thought, but you can run a church without God!

But the church isn't manmade. It is God-breathed. We can have a great show, a high-powered staff, and all the fancy marketing in the world, but if God doesn't blow wind in the sails, it's not going to matter throughout eternity.

I think that a reasonable plan and a decent amount of talent can attract a crowd. But it won't build a church. I think it's possible to launch a church, gather a bunch of people, and build some effective ministries *all without God*. You can make a name for yourself, gather a bunch of blog readers and teach God's Word *all without the power of God*.

Piper is right. There's a big difference between a motorboat and a sailboat.

If you want to start a cool church, with trendy music and casual dress, you can do that without God's help. Magazines or college students can help you become cool. Hiring a band can result in good music. You can steal some good sermons from the Internet and fool your people. But if you want to see genuine life change, if you want to be a part of building the Kingdom, if you want a ministry that is bigger than yourself, then it has to begin in the heart of God.

CONFIRMING THE CALL

If God is calling you to plant a church, then he will also confirm that call. God called Moses, and then he proved it by turning his staff into a snake. God called Gideon, and he proved it to him with the fleece. Jesus called Peter, and even after his denial, he confirmed the call by telling him to feed the sheep.

As a church planter, I think there are at least two areas where God will confirm your call.

Gifts

You know the age-old story of the lady in the church who feels called to sing on the platform. She loves Jesus. She learned the song. She's committed to her church. But she just can't sing. A lot of churches will let her sing on the stage because *her heart is in the right place.* But the people in the audience are not listening to her heart. They are suffering because of her really bad voice.

She may think she's been called to sing, but the problem is that she hasn't been gifted. And you're probably not gifted to like bad karaoke.

The first few episodes of American Idol are always the best to me because I like to watch the train wrecks. I feel sorry for people, but I still laugh at them. How in the world did they think they could make it as a singer? And even if they had somehow disillusioned themselves into thinking they had talent, why would their friends and family allow them to make fools out of themselves?

Why didn't someone, long before Simon, sit them down and tell them that while their heart and passion were great, their voice just didn't match?

In the same way, I truly believe that there are a lot of committed Christians and ministers out there who were not gifted to be church planters. They mistake a passion for the church with a call from God to launch one.

In *15 Characteristics of Effective Pastors*, Kevin W. Mannoia and Larry Walkemeyer, argue that Godly character *and* ministry competence make an effective pastor.

You may disagree with me, but I believe there are two primary gifts or talents that you're going to need in order to launch a successful church: communicating and leading. If you are going to stand before a group of people each weekend, then you need to be good at it. You can get better with time, but if you don't have a decent amount of ability to begin with, you're never going to become great. I apologize if this sounds too much like a Simon-critique, but most of the time, Simon is right. I think a teacher needs to be called to teach God's Word, but I think he should also be good at it.

The other primary talent that church planters need is leadership. You need to know how to inspire people to action. You're going to lead a staff and lead a group of volunteers. I have a pretty simple test for leadership, and it comes in the form of a question. Do people follow you? I've never met a leader that didn't have any followers!

Other People

Another way God may confirm his call on your life is through the relationships that you have with other people. Do people see something in you? Do they affirm the fact that you would be good at it?

A few of the churches I worked in had "youth Sunday," when the youth group got to take over and all the adults endured loud music. Sometimes, I would be given the opportunity to teach adults. I was always encouraged when people would come up to me after the service and say "good job." I know some of them were just being polite, but I could tell that a few people actually meant it.

When I was nineteen years old, a church called me and asked me to come speak at their church on a Sunday morning. I drove about 40 miles and was the speaker for a revival. I remember one lady came up to me after the service, put her hand on my shoulder and told me that I would be a great pastor one day. I don't think she meant that I totally stunk that day; I think she was trying to affirm the call of God on my life. I don't remember that lady's name, or even the name of that church, but I remember what she told me.

This whole concept of affirming the call is one reason that I try to point out gifts and abilities in people that I meet. When I see something in someone I try to tell them. Because you never know what God is saying to them privately, and you never know what the future might hold for them.

It's Not Enough to Love Jesus

The fact that you're called to plant a church will not automatically mean that your church will be successful. Loving Jesus and being called is not enough. There are a lot of people with great hearts who love Jesus and have great families who will accomplish very little in life. The Apostle Paul says in Philippians 2:12 that we have to work out our salvation with fear and trembling. In the same way, I think we have to work out our calling.

As a church planter, there will be days that make you want to quit. There will be times when it just seems like too much work. The offering will not be enough to pay the bills and you'll get a phone call that one of your most committed core group members is going to start attending another church because they have more for teenagers. You're going to get frustrated with staff. You're going to feel far away from friends and family. You're going to second guess the location. You are going to wonder if the right people are around you. You're going to feel like quitting. And through all of this, you're going to stay faithful, suck it up and strap it on, because God has called you to the fight.

CHAPTER 2:
A BLOG, A CONFERENCE, AND A COACHING NETWORK

You'll never be ready to start a church.

When I left behind a dozen years in youth ministry, I was excited, but I wasn't prepared. I had no idea how to lead adults. I had no idea how to write bylaws or handle church finances. I absolutely hated visiting people in the hospital and doing weddings. I didn't know if I could lead a staff, much less a staff that would probably be older than me.

As a thirty-one-year-old, I didn't even know if people would show up to a church that was pastored by a guy like me. On top of that, I wasn't connected to a bunch of other church planters. I didn't know famous people in ministry. I couldn't name-drop, and I didn't have a blogroll. At the time that I'm writing this chapter, I'm two years into the church-planting journey, and I still have very little idea about what I'm doing. I still don't think I'm ready!

But as I looked back on other key moments in my life, I realized that I wasn't ready for most of them.

I dated quite a few girls through high school and college, and I almost always had a girlfriend. Then I graduated from college and went to seminary. I realized that if I was going to get serious about this ministry thing, I needed to focus my energy on learning. So I decided that I wasn't going to pursue any relationships at all. As soon as I made this groundbreaking decision, I went down to Florida to be a groomsman in my old college roommate's wedding.

I'm a pretty short guy, just five-seven, so I was matched up with the shortest bridesmaid. Jennie is a tiny bit shorter than five feet tall, and we walked down the aisle together. On the way to the reception, I told a friend of mine that I had just met the girl I was going to marry. He thought I was nuts.

I called Jennie up out of the blue and asked her out on a date. I'd never done that kind of cold-call dating before, but she said yes. It was probably not a good idea to go out on a double date with the couple that had just gotten married and had been back from their honeymoon for just a few days, but that's what we did. We went to a Japanese steakhouse and then went to play miniature golf.

A couple of years later, I asked Jennie to marry me. I was through college, partly through seminary, and didn't have much money in the bank. I didn't know how to be a husband. You might say that I wasn't really prepared for marriage. I had no idea what marriage would be like, but that didn't keep me from tying the knot. Looking back on that moment, I wasn't ready, and I had a ton of questions. But I'm glad that I went forward.

Anyone who tells you they are prepared for marriage is a liar.

Three years into our marriage, we found out that we were pregnant. I'm not sure why people say *we,* because the pregnancy really belonged to Jennie. We weren't trying to have kids and we weren't really ready. We had just gotten used to being married, and now there was going to be a kid in the mix.

When Jennie took the pregnancy test, she told me the news with tears in her eyes. I raced to the drugstore to buy some more pregnancy tests. I got three or four of them, just to be safe. I remember asking the lady at the store, "What's the most expensive pregnancy test you have?" Jennie took more tests, and they all came back the same. But just to be safe, we went to the doctor and had a blood test done. Of course, the blood test confirmed what the $67 worth of home tests told us—we were about to be parents.

I didn't know the first thing about car seats, baby food, or paying for college, but we were thrust into the world of parenthood. I wasn't prepared at all. But a few months later, our first child was born, and all that fear flew right out the window. My lack of experience really didn't matter once I laid eyes on Lauren.

Looking back on both of these experiences, I wouldn't trade them for the world. The fact that I wasn't prepared didn't really matter. In fact, the lack of preparation took a backseat to the reality of the relationship.

Becoming a pastor is like becoming a parent. I'm not sure you can ever be ready for it. I don't think you are ever prepared. I said it before and it's worth saying again: I *still* don't feel prepared for this thing.

MORE THAN INFORMATION

When Andrew first met Jesus, the first thing he did was go out and find his brother. I wonder what would happen if Andrew met Jesus in some of today's churches. His road map would have looked a little different. Maybe something like this:

1. Attend a new Christians class
2. Attend a membership class
3. Join a Sunday school class or a small group
4. Sign a disciple covenant
5. Attend the men's breakfast on Thursdays at 6:00 a.m.

In Christianity, we've turned the path to discipleship into an educational process. It's become less a matter of the heart and more a matter of the head. The goal of the sermon on Sunday is to communicate information. We believe that the best Christians are the smartest Christians. It has become less about what you do and more about what you know.

I Corinthians 8:1 says, "Knowledge leads to pride." Some of the worst Christians in the world are some of the smartest Christians in the world. They know everything the Bible says, but they actually do very little of it. In the church today, our problem is not a lack of information, it's a lack of application.

One reason we don't have Sunday-night or Wednesday-night services at Oak Leaf Church is because our people don't need the information that comes from more sermons. What if we just lived out one sermon instead of trying to cram in three? The Bible is pretty clear that it's not what you know but what you do that really matters. John 13:35 says other people will know we are Christians by the love that we show one another, not by how smart we are, how many Bibles we own, or how many Beth Moore study groups we've led.

Knowledge might be a step in the discipleship process, but it's not the *final* step. As a youth pastor, I constantly reminded my students that spiritual maturity is not measured by age. I've seen eighteen-year-old high school students accomplish more for the Kingdom of God than forty-year-old Christians. I've seen junior high students live the Christian life better than sixty-year-old deacons. Faith is not measured by how old you are or how much you know.

In the same way that we have institutionalized the path to following Christ, we've turned ministry into a degree program. Just like many Christians are herded through a discipleship process, those that indicate they have a desire to go into full-time ministry are sent on a similar path.

Consider Jim. He's a seventeen-year-old high school senior that feels like God wants him to pursue a life in ministry. Jim goes and talks to his pastor who encourages him to go away to Bible College. Jim graduates from high school and goes to Bible College, where he learns about ministry in a classroom environment. He takes an evangelism class, where he's required to share his faith with ten people, but most of his learning comes from taking notes. Throughout his college years, there are seminary representatives who keep showing up, promising to prepare Jim for a life in ministry.

He graduates from Bible College and goes away to get a master's degree at a seminary in another state. Three more years of classroom experiences will prepare Jim for ministry in a local church.

Throughout this seven-year educational process, Jim gets a little hands-on experience at the small church he attends. He teaches a junior high Sunday school class and chaperones a lock-in. He wants to reach people with the Gospel, even though he's completely surrounded by other professional Christians and doesn't know many lost people.

After graduation, one of the departments at the seminary helps Jim prepare his resume. They even send it out to churches that are looking for staff members. He gets his first paying job at a church as a youth pastor.

Three months into being a youth pastor, Jim realizes that the classroom education didn't really prepare him for how to deal with parents, how to keep the financial secretary off his back, and how to get along with his pastor, who seems to have dramatically different ideas on how church should be. Jim struggles through ministry philosophy and staff relations. He feels like he's on a ministry island. It doesn't help that students, parents, and his pastor all pull him in different directions. Twelve months later, Jim decides that he's not cut out for ministry and sends his resume to local schools, hoping to get a job teaching English.

By the way, this story could just have easily involved a schoolteacher. They will consistently tell you that their years in the classroom didn't adequately prepare them for their first year of teaching.

Our quest for knowledge has tricked us into thinking that those who are the best educated will be the most successful in ministry. There are many churches that worship the degree. But if I need an electrician at my house, I don't want an electrician that has been to school or read some books; I want an electrician with experience. I don't want a plumber who knows the theory of pipes; I want one that knows what he's doing.

I am not saying that education is a wasted effort. I'm glad that I went to college. Seminary can help you understand God's Word. But a college degree or a seminary degree won't *automatically* prepare you for real-life ministry. If you're hanging your hopes on a classroom experience, that classroom experience is going to let you down.

BOOKS

We are blessed to live in a day where there is an abundance of information on church planting. Twenty years ago, there weren't as many resources available for people thinking about starting a new church. But pioneer churches have paved the way for you and I to learn.

Some of the best books that you can read on the subject of church planting do not talk about church planting at all—they are business and marketing books. We will talk about marketing in chapter six, but business and marketing books will help you start a church. When I moved to Cartersville, I didn't know much about advertising, but I made it my mission to learn. I knew that I was starting a church, but I realized that there were many similarities to starting a business. I wanted everyone within driving distance to come to Oak Leaf Church, so I decided to become our Chief Marketing Officer.

BLOGS

Blogs are the new books because their content is fresh and up-to-date. Use Google Reader or Bloglines, and have fresh content delivered each day. Instead of visiting dozens of sites, you can read posts from the blogs you track in a few minutes each day. Blogs are a great way to learn about church planting, not to mention leadership and technology.

You can find church planting resources at *heretolead.com*, where I write about the behind-the-scenes stuff that happens at Oak Leaf Church. We also make resources, handouts, and series graphics available for download. We talk about the tools and sites that we use in our church.

CONFERENCES

I like what Perry Noble, the senior pastor of NewSpring Church in Anderson, South Carolina has to say about conferences.

> *The Bible says in Proverbs 4:6-8 that we need to get wisdom–NO MATTER WHAT IT COSTS US!*
>
> *I've been a FREAK about learning and growing from day one! We were spending money to bring in consultants the first year we existed as a church. I remember loading up a plane FULL of people in 2003 to take them to C3…and it RADICALLY changed the way many of them viewed ministry.*
>
> *I've always been "that guy" who, when given an opportunity to learn, stretch and grow, would get on a*

plane to WHEREVER and pay WHATEVER to learn. If you want to learn and grow...then there are PLENTY of opportunities to do so...you just have to pull your head out of your rear end for long enough to know that people aren't just going to give you everything you ask for...learning will cost.

The second sort of piggy backs off of the first...those who are willing to pay the price will grow...and those who complain about how much things cost and cry about things...you will stay EXACTLY where you are (unless you go backwards.)

I STUDY church planters like crazy because I want to learn from them...I believe the guys just beginning are some of the most creative and innovative people on the planet...and the ones getting it done, the ones making a difference, ALL OF THEM–they are absolute FREAKS about going to the right places and connecting with the right people. They pay for plane tickets, hotel rooms, meals...WHATEVER it takes if they believe it will make their church more effective for God's Kingdom.

Everything isn't free...so SHUT UP about paying money when Jesus actually gave His life!!![3]

I would also recommend that you go to a conference that's out of your comfort zone. Check out the "Together for the Gospel Conference" or the "HOW Design Conference." If you can't stand anything purpose driven, go sign up for one of their conferences and go with an open mind. If you're a lead pastor, attend a children's ministry conference (your children's ministry volunteers will love that). The purpose of attending conferences is to be challenged and exposed to new ideas. Try something new and different, and see what you learn.

---

[3] http://www.perrynoble.com/2008/01/15/what-i-wish-someone-would-have-told-me-part-two/

CONVERSATIONS

One of my favorite parts of attending a conference is the conversation that happens in the hallways. So much so that I've even thought about organizing a conference where there were no speakers or worship bands—just hallway and roundtable conversations. I'd call it the anti-conference.

I really learn a lot from meeting with people and asking questions. Guys like Brian Bloye, Shawn Lovejoy, Chunks Corbett, Mike Linch, Perry Noble, Tony Morgan, and Matt Willmington have all guided me into some good decisions. Their counsel has really helped us as a church, and we would not be where we are without their guidance. All of our staff members have connections with people that do their job in different places.

If you want to learn how to plant a church, ask someone who has planted a church. There's no shortage of opinionated church planters out there! In fact, I'd caution you to run all the advice you're given through your own filter and only believe 50 percent of what they tell you.

Write some specific questions down in advance. And when you go meet with church planters, don't do all the talking. Don't tell them about your carefully crafted prospectus. Ask questions, and then be quiet. If you're willing to learn, it's amazing how many opportunities you'll find.

And most high-level leaders write books or blogs, so you don't have to get coffee with them to learn from them.

INTERNSHIPS

Clark Howard is a cheapskate with a radio show. He's on AM radio in Atlanta and helps people "save more, spend less and keep from getting ripped off." People call in with their stories and questions, and Clark gives financial advice. I know I'm getting older, because I actually like listening to his show.

One afternoon, a guy called up his show and told Clark that he was thinking about getting into the fast food business. He wanted to transition from his current job and buy a franchise. He had investigated a few of the franchise opportunities that were available to him, and was calling to ask Clark for some advice.

Clark Howard told the guy that he should quit his current job and go work for one of the local restaurants. "Just get a job as a cashier," Clark said. Since this guy didn't know the ins and outs of the business, this would be a great way to learn things from an insider perspective. Since he wasn't in the fast food industry, working behind the counter or in the stock room would be great experience. After working there for six months he would be in a better position to make a good decision. The guy really wanted to start his business faster, and he didn't really like Clark's advice.

Proverbs 19:2 says that passion without knowledge leads to bad decisions.

I think a lot of church planters are passionate. We're locked, loaded and ready to go. We have strong ideas and big plans. We could go from thinking about starting a church to having our first service in about three weeks. But sometimes, the wise thing to do is to slow down, and seek knowledge before we act.

One of the best decisions I ever made in launching Oak Leaf Church actually slowed our launch down. We knew we were coming to Atlanta, and during my investigations, I got connected with West Ridge Church in Dallas, Georgia. Matt Willmington, their executive pastor asked me to come be one of their two church planting interns. I would hang out with the staff and learn things from the inside. I'd be doing what Clark Howard advised this potential restaurant operator.

I moved to Cartersville in April of 2005, and in August of that same year, I began my internship at West Ridge Church. My original plan was to launch the church on Easter of 2006, but the internship meant that I would have to push the launch date to the fall. Honestly, I felt like I *could* have launched a church without the support of West Ridge Church, but looking back, I'm so glad that I took the year to go through their program. I learned a lot and developed some great relationships. Matt Willmington now serves on our Board of Directors, and we still look to West Ridge Church for advice. They are our mother church, and we're proud of them. Hopefully, they are proud of us, too.

One of my prayers for Oak Leaf Church is that we will be a teaching church. I'm praying that someone will give us a house that we can turn it into an Intern House, so people can learn ministry on the job.

COACHING NETWORKS

My time at West Ridge Church was part internship/part coaching. They have a church planting school that meets one Saturday a month and goes through some great material. While the content was good, being part of the network was better. I got to spend half a day with other church planters in a learning environment. Though the church plants coming out of that network are all different, we had a common bond.

It seems like there are coaching networks popping up all over the place, and I'd encourage you to check them out. You can join a formal network, like the ones hosted by Nelson Searcy at *churchleaderinsights.com*. My friends at Mountain Lake Church also offer coaching. Check them out at *churchplanters.com*. Or you can develop your own network of church planting friends. Either way, I highly recommend that you become part of a network.

In January of 2008, I was a part of a pastor's roundtable. A group of about ten of us met for a couple of days without much of an agenda. We talked about small groups, multi-site strategy, budgeting, staffing, advertising, outreach and a bunch of other topics. The guys in this group are located all over the Southeast, but are leading similar style churches that are growing and reaching people. Tons of good ideas were shared, and we were able to encourage each other and have a good time. I think these kinds of events should happen more often.

In 2009, I started coaching a group of twelve church planters. They all say the experience was worth the investment, and I've learned a lot in the process. I believe a coaching network is the best place to learn about church planting.

TRIAL AND ERROR

I've learned the most about church planting by planting a church. No matter what the books, blogs, and conferences say, it's different when it's real. We learned how to plant a church by planting a church.

Greg Oraham, lead pastor of Foothills Community Church in Seneca, South Carolina says,

> *Most of it was trial and error. A few years before planting Foothills Community Church, we helped start*

another church in 1992. We basically had no clue what we were doing. I was familiar with Rick Warren and Saddleback's model to some degree back then, but we weren't sure how to implement it, but somehow God blessed, and the Church is thriving today. No doubt, I probably learned more about what NOT to do from this experience!

People cautioned me against starting too much too soon, but we still went ahead with trying to launch a monthly "believers service." The books and blogs all cautioned against doing too much too soon, but I still had to learn for myself.

THE TOOTHPASTE EFFECT

Just like you'll never know what it's like to be married until you're married, or what it's like to be a parent until you have kids, you'll never truly know what it's like to be a church planter until you're doing it. You won't feel prepared before you jump off, and you won't feel like you know what you're doing in the middle of it.

All of the great information that is out there might have the opposite affect on you. There are so many plans and ideas, and many of them are diametrically opposed to each other. One blog will tell you that the only thing you should care about is reaching lost people. Another will tell you that if you're not preaching expositionally through the Bible, then you're not doing it right.

Have you ever shopped for toothpaste? You've got whitening or tartar control. You can have bursts of mint or vanilla. There's Scope mouthwash built right into one, but the other is longer lasting. It's really enough to hope that your teeth all fall out. Chances are, you either teach yourself not to care, or you just don't buy toothpaste.

In the same way, all the church planting models out there can confuse you. That's why it's important to rest in the call of God and to know your area. What works in one city and what's taught at one conference might not work in your area.

And the last thing the Church needs is another Andy Stanley knockoff. And Christianity already has a great Bill Hybels.

Steven Furtick, the lead pastor of Elevation Church in Charlotte, North Carolina, says this:

> *Effective and lasting ministries are not built by cutting and pasting. They are birthed from the inside out. Sometimes we indiscriminately gather various components of different features of the body of Christ…an ear from one church, a nose from the other…and slap it all together like so. As a result, we don't wind up building much of a ministry at all. We wind up building a Frankenstein.[4]*

A BLOG FAST

In March of 2008, I decided to go on a month-long blog fast. I get a ton of good ideas from blogs, but I sensed I was relying too much on other people, and not enough on God.

For one month, I didn't read a blog or a leadership book. I intentionally cut off other voices so I could focus on the voice of God. I prayed and read my Bible more than ever.

In that month, God really spoke to me in some key areas. And I had a confidence that it was a word from the Lord, not just the advice of a friend. For leaders, I believe it's important to hear from God before hearing from men. As a pastor, I don't want to lead my church the same way another pastor leads their church. I want our direction to come from God, not from blogs.

I want our church to be a sailboat, not a motorboat.

Missionaries understand the concept of contextualization, putting a truth or principle in context of the people or culture that you are trying to reach. For church planters, this means that while you can and should learn from all the great leaders out there, you shouldn't try to become one of them. We shouldn't cut from their sermons or their ministries and paste them into our own settings.

I don't want to be the pastor that struggles to hear God's voice because I have too many other people's voices in my head.

---

[4] http://www.stevenfurtick.com/uncategorized/mr-potato-head-ministry/

Whether it's a book or a blog, a conference or a conversation, an internship or a network—learn all you can. Gather knowledge to go with your passion. Do your best to become an expert. But rely on God. Listen to his voice.

And in the end, realize that even with all that, you'll never feel fully prepared or qualified.

CHAPTER 3:
OTHER CRAZY PEOPLE

We didn't know a single person in Cartersville when we loaded up the U-Haul and moved there. This wasn't a big deal to me, because I'm an introvert and I don't like talking to people. Yeah, that's a pretty strange thing for a pastor.

My wife had just given birth to our second child and we moved with a three-week-old baby into a town where we didn't have friends or family. I knew I would meet people in the course of launching the church, but my wife was a stay-at-home mom with a three-year-old and a newborn and no help.

Even though it was forty-five minutes away, we wanted to get connected to a church, so we started attending West Ridge Church. We joined a small group, because we wanted to develop some relationships. My wife looked forward to those adult conversations every Wednesday night.

When our newest daughter was about three months old, we participated in one of West Ridge Church's baby dedication services. As we were sitting in the audience, waiting to go up on the stage, we overheard a conversation that was taking place in the row behind me.

A couple that was also dedicating their child, was talking to another couple. *We just started coming to West Ridge and we love it, but now we're going to have this whole new decision to make with the whole Oak Leaf thing.* My wife elbowed me.

Since I was going to be the lead pastor of the "whole Oak Leaf thing," I turned around and introduced myself. This couple was from Cartersville and had heard about our future church plant. We wouldn't have a service until more than a year later, but Kevin and Carrie Black became our first core group members.

A few weeks later, West Ridge introduced me and a few other church planters during a service. After the service, a couple came up to me and said they lived in Cartersville, and they would love to be a part of a church like West Ridge that was closer to home. Robby and Julie Reeves became our second core group family.

Not much happened for the next few months. I visited a few church plants on Sunday mornings and started working on a bunch of documents. In August, I began my official internship at West Ridge.

In October of 2005, we had an Informational Meeting in Cartersville. I spent $75 and rented a meeting room at a hotel, and I hung up a sign at the UPS store. That night, six families (including the two I'd already mentioned) showed up. I talked about the vision for the church and described what I thought it would look like.

The next week, we decided to start meeting on Sunday nights at Kevin and Carrie's home. The core group was official.

For the next few months, anywhere from six to twelve people would meet. Someone would occasionally bring in a new person, and sometimes, they would even come back. We talked about our core values and dreamed together about what Oak Leaf Church would look like.

In February, we moved the core group to a little larger location and we changed our name. The core group became the launch team, and our meetings now included a little planning.

We continued to meet until the summer. We worked on community outreach projects, visited other churches together and started planning Sundays.

We did a practice service in June, and a preview service in July. The Grand Opening service was August 20, 2006. The Launch team disbanded—mission complete.

WHERE DID WE GET PEOPLE

I already told you about the two couples that joined us from West Ridge. Here's where the rest of the people came from:

- We picked up one or two free agents from around the town. These are a few people I met along the way. I'd meet them to talk about the vision and values of the new church, give them the sales pitch, and invite them to our launch team meetings.
- A guy named Ryan heard about what we were doing from another member of our launch team. He called us up out of the blue. Ryan helps with the setup team, plays in the band and is an all-around great help.
- Brad and Tiffany found out about Oak Leaf Church from a friend. They started attending our launch team and Brad offered to let us use his sound system. I'm always skeptical of people in Georgia who say they have sound systems because this usually means they have things in their garage purchased at Radio Shack. But Brad had some serious sound gear, and he let the church use it for nearly a year. We eventually bought it from him. The Nash family was an answer to prayer.

All in all, there were about twenty-five adults and twenty children on our launch team. We didn't have a bunch of people come from another church. I didn't have a bunch of relationships from the area. God just brought who he wanted.

CHRISTIANS OR NON-CHRISTIANS?

Oak Leaf Church would focus on reaching people who were far from God, but I realized that we would need some believers to help us start. I did not *pursue* Christians who were actively involved in other churches, but I did not set out to build a launch team only with nonbelievers.

Some great people came to us from some other churches. They didn't come with attitudes or agendas; they came because they wanted to be a part of a church that would reach people. While our church is passionate about reaching people who do not attend church or who are far from God, we are not antagonistic toward other Christians who want to be a part of that vision. Over the course of our first couple of years, I met dozens of Christians who told me they had been praying for a church like ours to come to Cartersville. Be careful when you say who your church is for; the church isn't for Christians, and the church isn't for lost people. The church is for God; it belongs to Him. Maybe He should have some say on who is there.

I didn't want to tell God who could be a part of our launch team. I didn't want to decide in advance who He wanted to join us. I made it known that we were not targeting Christians from other churches, but when they came to us with the right attitude and in the right way, they were welcomed with open arms.

HEARTACHE

One of my biggest heartaches in the launch team phase was meeting people, pouring my heart out to them, and watching them decide not to be a part of what we were doing. There were many lunches and dinners where I talked about vision to people who decided to go elsewhere.

I know we're all on the same team, but don't let anyone tell you that this isn't a big deal. I was (and still am) convinced that Oak Leaf Church is hands-down the best church in this town. I wanted everyone to be a part, and I couldn't understand why anyone wouldn't want to be a part of this church plant. I'm a Kingdom player, but I wanted everyone to buy into what we were doing. Seeing someone encounter our vision and decide not to join the team is like having someone meet your children and tell you they are ugly. The church was my baby, and it hurt to see a few people walk away.

If you've been through the launch team phase, you know what I'm taking about. If you're not there yet, go ahead and gear up for it. There will be key people that leave, and it will hurt. Someone will surely tell you not to take it personally, but that's impossible. Of course your church plant is personal to you.

A CHANGE IN TERMINOLOGY

We started with a core group but transitioned into a launch team. The terminology is important. *Core group* implies internal development; *launch team* indicates activity.

During the core group phase, we talked exclusively about the vision and values of the church. For seven weeks in a row, we went through the Scriptural basis for our core values. I'd talk an entire week about *truth*, and how this value would flesh itself out on Sunday mornings and throughout the week. We talked about what *excellence* really meant. We talked about *community* and how we would be a church of small groups.

This early focus on small groups really helped the core group understand who we were going to be as a church, but it was also my first opportunity to verbalize our values in somewhat of a teaching setting. It's one thing to have values on a sheet of paper, but it's another thing to discuss them in real life.

During this core group phase, we met in a living room. It was relaxed and informal. All of our kids hung out in a basement. After about three months I told everyone, "Guys, the core group is officially disbanded—you are now a part of our launch team."

During the launch team phase, we met in a different location. One of our members owned a dance studio and she allowed us to meet there. Our discussions took a little different form.

- Occasionally, we'd bring someone in to lead worship with an acoustic guitar. We met potential worship leaders for our weekend services this way.
- Our children met in one of the other studio rooms, and we actually tested the children's curriculum that we were thinking about using.
- I continued to talk about vision, but I also added a little more "Bible study" to the mix.
- We spent a lot of time talking about the specifics. How do we want to setup the facility? Who would work with children? Who would work as greeters? Everyone on the launch team would have two or three jobs once we began meeting on Sunday mornings.

- We planned out some community outreach events – everybody always had a job.
- We placed offering baskets at a makeshift information table so people could give.
- On Easter, we celebrated communion together.

VISITING OTHER CHURCH PLANTS

During the spring and early summer, we would visit other churches and church plants together. Our people were like private investigators. They would go into a church plant, check-in their children, sit through the service, and meet people. They would take notes, and we'd all bring those notes to our meeting that night. We would talk through what we liked and what we didn't like. We talked about what signs we noticed and what made us feel funny.

These days, it seems like there is always a church planter or a church planting team at one of our services. I love that, because it's a great way to learn. We love it when church planters come to visit our service, and we always give them a backstage tour and take time to answer their questions. We learned so much from visiting other churches, and we hope we can help people when they visit.

PLANNING THE PREVIEWS

As it got closer to the summer, we turned our attention from evaluating other churches to getting ready for our own preview service. We had originally planned to do three preview services—one in May, one in June and one in July. But since we couldn't find a location to meet, we had to cancel the May preview service.

During the month of May, we got the confirmation that we would be able to hold Sunday services in the brand new movie theater in town. Our team sprang into action to get ready for that first preview service.

First, there was the implementation of the service itself. From the beginning, we decided that excellence meant we would have to work hard to set things up right. We weren't just going to set a drum kit on the floor of the theater—we wanted a full stage. We had to move legs around on our staging to get the pieces to fit in the room.

Then, we had to get the word out. We didn't have a lot of money, so we focused on word of mouth advertising. I challenged our small launch team to spread the word. We printed up one hundred road signs that simply read "Church at the Movies—oakleafchurch.com" and put them around town on the weekends. We scraped together enough money to do a five thousand-piece mailout. Looking back on it all, that's kind of laughable. We would have done a larger mailout, but we didn't have the money. I'll talk more about direct mail in chapter six.

We had a great sound system, and we scraped together about $2,000 for children's ministry equipment. But we still didn't have any lights, and we didn't have a worship leader.

BRINGING IN BANDS

I called my friend Tim Combs, who was the road manager for a band named Tenth Avenue North. I had met these guys during my youth ministry days and they had played at several camps and retreats for me. For $500, they came to Cartersville and led worship for us at our first two preview services. To top things off, they brought their lighting kit. These guys have since signed a record deal with Reunion Records.

In fact, for the first three months of our church's existence, we didn't have a worship leader. We just booked bands and brought in different people to lead. We never told our people that these were semi-professional musicians – we just called them the Oak Leaf Band! We knew we needed to have excellent music, and if we didn't have the people in our church, we'd just fake it.

The strategy of bringing in bands worked great for us, and I'd highly recommend it. Here's what the strategy did for us:

- It allowed us to have quality music from day one.
- It attracted good musicians. Talented musicians will not attend a church with mediocre music. In just a short time, we realized that we had some pretty talented musicians coming to our church. Today, our band is made up of volunteers from within our church.

- It allowed us to save money. I called in favors and found local bands. When you think about it, paying a band each week comes out to be about what most people would pay a full-time worship leader. I really believe that this strategy gave us more bang for the buck.
- It allowed us to staff in other areas. We focused our staff on community outreach, small groups and children's ministry.

We booked bands that seemed to match our style. I would ask them for a list of seven or eight songs that they liked playing, and I would narrow the list for them. That gave us some control over the set list, but still allowed the band to play what they knew.

A different worship leader on stage each week wasn't an issue for us, because the style was similar each week. Now that we have a creative arts pastor on staff full-time, we still utilize other people on stage. It's part of our culture, not just in the music area, but also in the teaching area. In our first year as a church, I had other staff members or guest speakers teach eight different Sundays. We don't want our church to be driven by a single personality.

Chances are, you'll find some great musicians in your area. If there is a college campus nearby, I guarantee that there are some good worship leaders. You should visit every Christian campus group and meet college students. I even know a church planter on the West coast that found a worship leader on craigslist!

THE FIRST PREVIEW SERVICE

The first song ever played at Oak Leaf Church was "Salvation is Here" and the first message I ever delivered was on the prodigal son. I talked about the main character in that story – not the son, but the Father, who was just waiting for his child to come back home. The whole service was a snapshot of what our church is about – pointing people to Jesus and the grace and hope that He gives.

After the first preview service, one of our first core group members came to me and said, "That was the first time I ever heard you really preach. I'm glad you were decent."

After the preview services, our launch team got together and talk about all the things we needed to fix before the next service. Since teamwork was one of our core values, everybody really stepped up to make things better. To this day, we don't have a bunch of people in leadership positions at Oak Leaf Church that point out problems. Instead, our people are part of the solution.

On the wall in our office, we hang inspirational quotes and phrases. One of these says, "Everybody is smarter than somebody." That speaks to our core value of teamwork.

Between the two preview services, I learned a valuable lesson from Julie Reeves, one of our launch team members. I was planning to talk through our core values and vision at our second preview service. Julie said to me, "That's cool, but I was kind of hoping that you would just teach a real message. I have invited some friends and I'm sure they would love to experience what a real service would be like."

At that moment, I realized what preview services were supposed to be. They weren't opportunities to tell the community what we were *going* to do. They weren't opportunities to *talk* about the vision – they were opportunities to *be* the vision. Instead of telling people that our services would be funny, I should just be funny. Instead of telling people that we were going to have passionate, upbeat music, we should just play those kinds of songs. There are too many people that use the present to talk about the future, when God has given you a platform to make something out of today.

Julie taught me a valuable lesson that day. We needed to *be* the vision, not just have one.

FROM PREVIEWS TO GRAND OPENING

We received $2,000 in the offering that first preview service. I thought that was a huge offering. Another church also stepped up and gave us $5,000, and we used that money to buy a lighting system of our own. We spent money as fast as we got it and our bank account rarely had more than $1,000 in it.

For the grand opening, we did a "huge" mailout—ten thousand pieces! That's still funny to me. I know church planters that do multiple, forty thousand piece postcards to advertise their launch. Those guys still make me jealous.

We had 140 people attend our first preview service. There were 180 in attendance at the second preview. And there were about 250 people at our grand opening. I have no idea where these people came from. Remember, we didn't spend much money on advertising, and our launch team had about twenty-five people.

But God was good. I truly believe that much of the success during our first year is because of the faithful people who gave, served, and prayed. It's amazing to think that a church could grow from twenty-five to six hundred in one year, but throughout Scripture, God took a little and turned it into a lot.

CHAPTER 4:
BIG VISION TAKES BIG MONEY (OR DOES IT?)

I had a vision. I had a plan. I had a place. But I didn't have a lot of money. A dozen churches didn't line up to offer us financial support. And no denomination swept in to write us a fat check.

Let me make a confession: I'm just not wired for fundraising. Maybe it's because I don't like asking for help, or maybe it's because I'm not a salesman, or maybe it's for no good reason at all. But God didn't wire me to raise money.

About a year ago, I met a church planter that went to a big city. He was able to raise a ton of money through various connections. In fact, an organization gave him $250,000 to start a church. When I heard that story, I (selfishly) thought, "Man, imagine what we could have done with $250,000!"

Maybe I just hadn't learned the art of name-dropping, but we didn't raise anywhere near that much.

Between January 1, 2006 and our grand opening Sunday on August 20, 2006, we raised and spent about $55,000. That includes salaries, outreach events, rent for our preview services, bands, kids equipment, website and software costs, office space, and about one hundred other little things that you never think about in advance. I had a list of stuff we needed to buy, and whenever we got some money, we'd buy something. If we got a check on Monday, it was spent by Tuesday.

HOW MUCH WILL IT COST TO PLANT A CHURCH?

I get this question a lot. And over time, I've come up with a really simple answer to the question.

Question: How much is it going to cost to plant a church?

Answer: Everything you have.

If you raise $20,000, then that's how much it will cost. If you have $100,000 then it will cost that much.

I strongly believe that the success of your church plant should not be tied to money; it should be tied to the call of God and the wise decisions you make as the result of that call. I know church planters who are successful with less money than we had. I know church planters who have invested hundreds of thousands of dollars and didn't make it. Just like money isn't the solutions to problems in life, money isn't the solution to problems in church planting.

If you're struggling with fundraising, or if you don't have a lot of money, hopefully I can give you some freedom today. It's okay. There are those who will be given way more than you, but there are those who have planted great churches with less. God is bigger than the bank account.

You probably know the parable of the talents. The master who decided to leave town left a few people in charge of his finances. One guy got ten talents, another got five and the last guy got one. Two of three guys doubled the money, and one guy buried it in the ground.

The guy with the single talent is condemned; he's actually called wicked. But both of the guys who were faithful stewards were commended. I think it's interesting that both of the people who were successful started with a different amount of money.

It's not just about how much money you can raise, it's how you can leverage those God-given resources to advance the Kingdom. Some might be blessed with extraordinary fundraising abilities, or receive huge contributions from partnering churches, but that doesn't automatically translate into success. Don't fall into the comparison trap; just be faithful with what God has given you.

RAISING SUPPORT

Like most church planters, I raised support to cover my salary during the time when I was working on the foundational elements of the church. When we finally decided to act on the call of God to plant a church, I wrote a letter and sent it out to about one hundred people. I didn't ask them to pledge or give anything; it was just an update letter.

After we moved to Georgia, we sent another letter to those same people and asked them to financially partner with us. About a month later, I sent out a third and final letter.

As I went through the support-raising process, I learned three lessons:

1. The people who you think will give you money may not rush in to meet your needs. And those you send a letter to as a long shot just might help you. Ask everyone.
2. Most people don't help. It's not that most people don't agree with your vision, it's just that they won't personally buy in. Maybe they already give to their church. Maybe they have gotten ten letters like yours before. But the reality is that the majority of people you ask for support won't be able to help. It's just reality, and you should prepare for it.
3. Most churches already have their budgets committed to things and are having a tough time meeting that budget as it is. Most pastors offered to pray for me (I wonder if they did), but they said their church wasn't in a position to help. I realize that it's impossible to help every church plant that comes around asking for money, but it's still a downer to ask and be turned away.

Throughout the support process, I tried to do all the things that other people told me to do. Let me summarize some of the things that worked well for us.

1. Regular communication with supporters is important. Ben Arment, founding pastor of Reston Community Church in Reston, Virginia says fundraising was one of his greatest successes. "I sent out a full color, glossy newsletter filled with photos and wonderful stories to a growing mailing list during the first year. I emphasized that it was consistently mailed monthly; paper, not email; and filled with more photos than text." Ben didn't ask for money until a year later. People are not going to respond to one or two letters—they need to continually see the vision. They need to hear stories and be able to relate.

2. Have another church manage the finances. Early on, our sponsoring church handled all of our contributions. We didn't have any organizational or financial systems in place, and I wanted the accountability. So when people sent money, they made their checks out to West Ridge Church and they held the funds for us. I've seen several church plants get into trouble because they didn't have adequate financial systems in place. This is just another reason why it's good to have a mother church. If you don't have a sponsoring church that is close to you, consider hiring a small business accountant.

3. Let your core group/launch team give to the vision. Every Sunday night at our launch team meetings, we would set out a basket and allow our launch team to contribute. I kept them up to date on the things we needed to buy. I made the decision to let all the money contributed by members of the launch team to go directly to the ministry, not to my salary. If your launch team isn't giving to the new church, and you're trying to rely solely on outside support, you are going to have much bigger problems very soon.

Over and over again, I made sure our team knew that we didn't have thousands of dollars coming in from other churches and organizations. This thing would be financed by everyday people, all doing their part. Three years into this church plant, we still don't have millionaires in our church writing big checks; it's the faithful, consistent giving of a whole bunch of people that make the difference.

Raising support was tough. There was a lot of uncertainty and I had a lot of questions. It sounds overly spiritual and trite, but God just took care of us. We had set aside about three months worth of living expenses, and by the time that was gone, support started to come in.

We could have done better in this area, and looking back, I probably could have put some more time into fundraising. Maybe I let the fact that I'm not a natural fundraiser become an excuse. But God was good, and we had enough.

HIRING OTHER STAFF

The first person we hired was Tim. Tim's job was to manage small groups, but early on he was basically the pastor of everything I didn't do.

Tim joined our team because God called him to be a part of the vision. He actually resigned from his position at a church in our area, not even really knowing that he was coming on board with us. When Tim joined our staff in April, four months before our grand opening, he set out to raise support for his salary in the same way that I did. Somehow, he made it through those four months. Once the church started meeting every week, we were able to pay about half of Tim's salary, while he continued to raise support for the other half. Things continued this way for about eighteen months.

When people join the staff at Oak Leaf Church, they generally make less money than they did at their previous job. While we place a huge priority on taking care of staff, the reality of the situation is that the pie can only be divided so many ways. Tim, and many others made sacrifices on the front end in order to be a part of our team.

As the church grew, we began to increase the amount of money the church provided while support tapered off. By year two, all support raising had ended. We intentionally phased out the option of raising outside support so people could focus 100 percent of their time on ministry.

BI-VOCATIONAL PASTORS

I have great respect for pastors who work a part-time or a full-time job in addition to serving as a pastor. But if at all possible, I think you should avoid it.

It's hard to do two things well. I think most church planters are pretty driven (if you're not driven, you're probably going to have a hard time in this field). And driven people like to do things well. I knew that if I had a "day job" it would take away from my ability to prepare for the launch of this church. If you have a backup plan, are you really diving headfirst into church planting?

Worse yet, there was the possibility that it would dull my passion for church planting. I knew bi-vocational church planting wouldn't work for me.[5]

When I moved to Cartersville, we basically had about three months worth of living expenses. Like a poker player, we went all-in. I figured I had three months to get things going. If it came to it, I would get a job to pay the bills, but that would be the absolute last resort.

If you were a first-century fisherman, then your nets were your source of income. When the Bible describes Peter leaving his nets, that wasn't some symbolic action. Peter literally left behind his source of income; he left his job in order to follow Jesus.

I think it's best for a church planter to focus nearly all of his energy on launching the church. What task could be more important? If you don't have the money set aside, I would keep working and keep saving, so when it's time to step out, you can do so with both feet.

When I was a youth pastor, I co-founded a parachurch ministry called 412 Students. It later became Sidekick Students. We organized camps and ski trips and weekend events for youth groups. It got to the point where we were running multiple camps in the summer (I would speak at some of them). We never really made a lot of money doing this, but there was always this huge potential on the horizon. I'm convinced that I could have dived in headfirst and made the thing work.

But as a church planter, I had to make the decision to let a good thing die. During the ramp-up year, I continued to work with Sidekick Students. But once we started meeting every week, I realized that I didn't have the time or energy to do both things well. We finished out the events we had scheduled, and effectively shut it down. Jim Collins is right when he says that good is the enemy of great. I could keep things going and have a good camp ministry and a good church plant, or I could strategically say no and have a great church plant. For me, it all went back to the call of God. Speaking to students was good, but it wasn't the one great thing that God had called me to do.

---

[5] I know that Paul was a tent-maker, but he also talked about Christians supporting ministers so they could do the work of the ministry without hindrance.

> I think focusing on two or three things is the kiss of death for *some* church planters. Working another job might be the reason the church plant never takes root or takes off.

SETTING A BUDGET

Our first annual budget was a joke. I think I opened up Excel and changed it at least three times a week. No matter how many sample budgets you read, you won't have a clear picture of your financial situation. Your best attempt at a year one budget will be a guess, and chances are, it will be pretty far off base.

I made a start-up budget and included it in my prospectus, but it didn't match. I still chuckle to myself when I see startup budgets in prospectus documents that people send my way. I know we underestimated a bunch of areas in our first budget.

In year two, we did a little better. Our budget was halfway accurate, because we had a year's worth of numbers to use as a guide. We started to zero in on how much things really cost in our culture. Our budget started to look like the things we valued as a church.

I'm not saying that you should ignore the year one start-up budget. I'm just saying it doesn't matter as much as you think it does. Denominations and other groups will probably want to see that you have a plan, but I wouldn't spend too much time agonizing over the specifics.

Throughout the budgeting process, I learned a valuable principle. Percentages are better than numbers. While the numbers may change, if you set your budget according to percentages, then you can budget based off of your values. Here's how our 2009 budget broke down:

> **Staff: 45 percent.** This includes salaries, benefits, conferences, retreats, and staff travel expenses. Most churches we talked to tried to keep this number around 50 percent.
>
> **Facilities: 21 percent.** This includes the mortgage payment on the 15,000-square-foot nightclub that we purchased in 2008 and use for offices, student ministry and weekend services.

Ministry: 21 percent. This includes worship, kids ministry, student ministry, small groups, outreach events, and church planting support.

Administration: 13 percent. This includes database software, office supplies, membership fees and advertising. All the business stuff.

BUDGET BY VALUES

Once you set the percentages based on your values, then the numbers take care of themselves. As giving goes up, you know you have more to spend on staff and advertising. By working a budget off of percentages, you can also get other people involved in the discussion without them knowing actual numbers. Budgeting with percentages is also great for talking about the things you value as a church.

Should you spend more or less money on the weekend services? That's a value question, not a dollar question.

What percentage of our budget should we allocate to facilities? That's a value question, not a dollar question.

How much should we spend on advertising? Again, it's values, not available funds.

As your church grows, your values will determine your decisions. Make sure that you write down your organizational values and let those values guide your systems.

TALKING ABOUT MONEY

Depending on your church background, you probably have an opinion on teaching about money in the church. There are some that think it's a taboo subject—a turnoff to the post-modern generation that is skeptical of the church precisely because they focus on money too much.

And there are other churches that harp on money all the time. Somehow, a sermon about the Holy Spirit will turn into a challenge to tithe more. Ever heard a message with a progression of points like this?

1. God is love.
2. You should love others.
3. Loving others means serving others.
4. The best place to serve others is at church.
5. It costs a lot of money to operate the church.
6. By giving to the church, you're really serving others.
7. If you love God, you will tithe.

All of those statements can be true, but when every message turns into money, people start smelling the fish.

Like all things in life, I think there's a healthy balance when it comes to the subject of money. The fact of the matter is that Jesus talked about money more than he talked about heaven and hell combined. It's the number-two subject in the Bible (second only to love).

Don't avoid a subject just because it's misunderstood or abused. Teach on money appropriately, accurately, and passionately. When I look back at our teaching calendar (another resource that's available on *heretolead.com*), I realize that the eighth message in the history of Oak Leaf Church was about giving. In our ninth month as a church, we did an entire series on money. And our church actually grew in attendance during that series!

One time when I taught about money someone wrote a message to us on the offering envelope. It said, "Stop harping on money so much…maybe if you didn't have fancy lights then you wouldn't need more money. Just preach the word." There was nothing inside the offering envelope.

The only people that get mad when you talk about giving are the people who don't give. The bottom line is that giving is a heart issue, and as a pastor of a church your job is to help people follow Jesus with their whole heart.

Whenever we talk about giving, I remind our church that we hope there are two kinds of people at our church: those who are far from God, and those who are dialed-in disciples ready to serve. I challenge those who are a part of the body of Christ to step up to the plate and trust God with their finances, and remind those far from God that we do much of what we do for them.

People are not turned away when the church talks about money. The average unchurched person knows that it takes money to run a church. They know there are light bills and personnel expenses. They know that things aren't free. Unchurched people are turned off when pastors *abuse* the subject of money for seemingly personal gains.

Here are a few helpful hints on teaching about money in a church plant:

- Teach people how to manage their finances; don't just beat them up about giving. We get in trouble when we talk about the ten percent but forget to help people with the ninety percent. I am convinced that people in the church *want* to give, but they don't think they are able. Twice in our first two years as a church, we brought in Joe Sangl, a finance guru, to lead a "Financial Learning Experience." This one-time class is designed to help people get out of debt, live by a budget, and get their finances under control. If all of your money messages revolve around the tithe, then you're missing the larger principle of stewardship and management.
- Plan the offering like a service element. Use live stories, video stories, and tell people where the money goes. In our series planning we ask ourselves, "What are we going to do to emphasize the time of giving?" We plan out the offering just like we plan out songs or videos. There are a lot of creative and interesting things you can do that are much better than a person getting up on the stage and saying, "Now, we're going to have the offering." One of the defining moments in our church was the time we showed a video about the need for wells in Rwanda. The video talked about how far women would travel to find clean water and explained that for $3,000, an organization could build a well that would service an entire village. At the end of the video, I didn't tell people we were receiving a special offering. I told them that because of their faithful giving, we already sent a $3,000 check. Everyone in the room clapped! Our church was just three months old at the time, but our people were excited that we were making a difference around the world. In the appendix, you'll find fifty-two offering talk ideas that will make the time of giving in your church service far more meaningful.

- Balance being honest with being strong. I let people know that I give to our church. We don't talk about the specifics of the budget, but there are times to be honest. At the end of the year, I talk honestly about how giving was in the last year and how we set the budget for the next year. I talk about the budget in the context of vision and why we do what we do. I have never gone to our church and said, "We can't pay the light bill." But I have challenged our church to excel in giving so we could hire a full-time family pastor.
- Say thanks and let people know where they are. Most churches send out annual contribution statements with a letter from the pastor. I challenge you to communicate more often than that and connect the dots for people. Now, we send out quarterly letters, which are more like brochures highlighting what's happening in the church and thanking people for their financial gifts. We include a brief financial statement every time.

It seems like there's always a financial need. Once you navigate toward the launch, you'll really need to hire a staff member. Once you have the team in place, it will be time to move to a larger facility.

But don't let this spiritual principle just fall by the wayside. If God has called you to plant a church, and you're following Him, then He's going to take care of your needs.

If the church is a sailboat, God will provide the finances. Be faithful to lead the way God has called you to lead and trust that God will provide.

CHAPTER 5:
THE PIPES IN THE WALL

We built the second house we ever owned. By "we built," I really mean that someone built it and we got to pick out the colors. But we watched the house go up and we got to monitor the progress. Before they poured the driveway, I went out and laid a piece of PVC pipe down, so when I wanted to install an irrigation system, I wouldn't have to shoot a pipe under the driveway.

Even though it was technically against the builder's policy, I went into the house after it had been framed and before it had been dry walled and ran some audio cable through the walls. I wanted to install a surround sound system once the house was completed, and having some of the wires already in place would save a ton of time, energy and money.

I think church structure should be just like that section of PVC pipe or just like those speaker wires. Hidden and out of sight. Laid down below the surface to make things easier later.

Structure is very useful to a church, just like those wires were useful to my movie watching experiences. But nobody wants to see the wires on the outside of the wall. They should be hidden and out of the way.

Structures and boards shouldn't be overly visible to the average person in the church. Instead, they are designed to work behind-the-scenes. The mission and the vision should be the driving force behind any church, not policies, procedures, rules or regulations.

Structure should also be simple. It's not necessary to create a lengthy document to cover every conceivable circumstance that might arise in your church. Think of it like this. You must operate the way your bylaws say, but you're always free to do more.

For example, if your bylaws call for at least one annual business meeting, you could still choose to have more if necessary. But if you describe a monthly business meeting in your bylaws, then you're locked into those meetings. (Until Thomas Jefferson writes an amendment.)

Founding documents should be short and sweet. They should provide freedom for ministry. They should act as train tracks, not as the train conductor. I love the way that the bylaws of North Point Community Church begin:

> *An imperfect system filled with men and women of integrity will function far better than a perfect system filled with men and women who lack integrity.*

There's a document that recognizes that people are more important than systems, and that ministry is more important than structure.

Finally, structures should serve the church, not the other way around. I once visited a church where they had more than a dozen committees. When the youth pastor wanted to hire an intern, the personnel committee asked him to collect resumes. By the time they met with the finance committee and all the other people involved in the process, three months had gone by. Everybody who had submitted a resume was no longer available. That's a broken system, and a church that is handicapped by their own structure.

Let's talk through some of the organizational systems that you'll put into place, probably before you have a public service.

INCORPORATION

Oak Leaf Church, Incorporated existed as a corporation before we even moved to Georgia. Starting a corporation is a quick and easy process, and there are several organizations that can help you. First, if your church is going to be a part of a denomination or an association, they may be able to help you. Secondly, you could contact a corporate attorney that you know and he could take care of all the details. Thirdly, you can do what we did and utilize the power and speed of Google.

We found a company[6] that would handle the paperwork and file the necessary documents in the state of Georgia. I paid the $300 filing fees, and Oak Leaf Church became an official corporation in 2005.

NON-PROFIT STATUS

Creating a non-profit corporation is not the same thing as obtaining non-profit status from the IRS. You'll want to make sure this is done, because it's this status that means people can make tax-deductible contributions to your church. Until the organization obtains 501(c)(3) status, people can make donations, but they are not tax-deductible.

This can be a time consuming process. You could fill out IRS form 2793 yourself, but I would recommend getting an attorney or an accountant to take care of this. If your church is a part of a denomination or association, you might be able to fall under their non-profit status. This was the case for us, and it saved us a lot of time and more than one headache.

BANK ACCOUNT

Once the church is an official corporation, and you're given a federal tax ID number, you can open a bank account. I would go ahead and open the account, but as I wrote about in the last chapter, I would still funnel contributions through a sponsoring church. That added layer of accountability will help.

I highly recommend that the lead church planter *not* be the one to sign checks. Add an additional check signer to the account and make

---

[6] We used Hubco. You can find them on the web at http://www.inc-it-now.com. There are approximately 2,324,938 other organizations that will take care of your incorporation stuff.

sure someone else has their eyes on the finances. We do most of our bill payments online, and I don't even know the login information.

PROSPECTUS

A prospectus isn't a legal document, but it's an important document that will help communicate your vision and your plan. In some ways, a prospectus is a Christian business plan. You can download a PDF of our prospectus at *heretolead.com*.

A good prospectus contains:

- Biographical information on the church planter. Make it personal. Include a picture of you and your family.
- Demographic information on the area. Be sure to answer the question: Why does this area need a church?
- A purpose statement or mission statement. In *Making Vision Stick*, Andy Stanley says that a purpose statement should be short, sweet, and memorable. "A statement that is memorable but incomplete is better than a statement that is complete but forgettable," he writes. The mission of Oak Leaf Church is to lead people from where they are to where God wants them to be.
- A description of what the church will be like. We chose to highlight our core values.
- A timeline. People need to know when you're planning on launching. Nobody wants to support an organization that will *eventually* do something.
- A list of supporting organizations. Some people will decide to help based on who's already on board. If you are a part of organizations, associations or denominations, then let people know. We actually created two versions of our prospectus, one that highlighted my background with the Southern Baptist Convention, and one that downplayed it. I know—that was a little sneaky, and I did feel bad about it for about fifteen minutes. Paul says he became all things to all people, so I figured this was okay.

- A short statement of beliefs. Nobody is looking for a theological treatise, but they do want to see that you're not a nut.

BYLAWS

As a youth pastor, my bosses and various deacons always referred to the constitution and bylaws. This holy document described the necessary waiting period between a church vote and the implementation of a program. I think Benjamin Franklin wrote it.

Church bylaws can be confusing, and they can turn into sacred cows. In some churches, the bylaws are right up there with the Gospel of John and the Hymnal. And don't even get me started about the Baptist Faith and Message.

Before I describe our bylaws, let me give you a caution. Don't write your bylaws too soon. If you haven't officially started your church, you don't need bylaws. If you're church is less than one year old, you probably shouldn't write bylaws. You should spend your time figuring out how you are going to go over the top to serve your community, not debating whether or not your Board of Directors should have four or five members. By the way, our actual bylaws are included in the Docs & Forms package at *heretolead.com*.

It takes time to know your style and discover your DNA as a church. Our sponsoring church didn't even write bylaws until they were six or seven years old. We didn't write bylaws until we had more than six hundred people attending our church on a regular basis. If you write your bylaws too early, you will run the risk of crystallizing a system that might not work for you in the long term.

As we wrote the bylaws, we read documents from other churches. I read a couple of books about church structure. I investigated what the Bible said about elders. Our bylaws describe these three groups of people.

Board of Directors

I believe that the church is a business. It's not *just* a business, but it is a business.

Our structure here probably resembles corporate America a little more than it does most churches. While this might make some people uncomfortable, we believe this system would provide us with the necessary accountability but still allow for the flexible nature of a church plant. The Board of Directors is composed of four to eight senior pastors, executive-level pastors or people in Christian ministry that understand the operation and ministry of the local church.

The Board of Directors at Oak Leaf Church has two primary responsibilities. First, they set my salary. This was important to me as the lead and founding pastor of the church. I didn't want to pull my own salary out of thin air, and I feel like it's a little fishy to hire someone that sets my salary. At the conclusion of the year, our executive pastor prepares a report detailing our finances from the last year. We take a look at what other lead pastors in similar sized churches make. We look at giving trends. We take all this information, summarize it, and then email it to our Board of Directors. They recommend a number. A lot of emails are exchanged, and a consensus is reached. Our executive pastor works with the board on this. I stay out of the loop.

The Board of Directors is also the group that could fire me. In the event that I resign or am fired, the Lead Team would function as the search committee, and the Board of Directors would give their approval on the next lead pastor.

We have chosen not to place the position of lead pastor under the authority of a group of people in the church. There are too many pastors that cannot lead the way that God wants them to lead out of fear of a board of deacons. By trusting this responsibility to a group of other pastors, who love Jesus and love the church, we are keeping with the spirit of accountability found in the Bible.

If you look at the structure of many corporations and businesses in the United States, you'll find boards made up of other executives. These leaders often understand the business and the unique responsibilities that come with senior leadership. Other pastors understand the responsibilities of ministry, and they are in a perfect position to help guide the church.

This is just one of many leadership structures that we investigated. In the end, it fit our DNA. There are great churches that have elder systems. There are growing churches that have different types of boards. The Board of Directors works for us.

No matter how perfect the system, there will always be ways around it. The IRS has thousands of pages of policies, yet people still find ways to cheat on their taxes. Guys who are part of accountability groups still find ways to cheat the system and cheat on their wife. Even one of the disciples turned out to be a bad guy!

For us, accountability is more than a system or a flow chart. It's an attitude. Those who are around us know that we're not dictators or tyrants. We're not trying to build our own little kingdom in Cartersville. We're open and honest, and we shoot straight. Once people are around, they see this in action.

Staff

Oak Leaf Church is a staff-led church, and this is the second group of people described in our bylaws. The staff is responsible and accountable for the day-to-day operations of the church.

As the lead pastor of Oak Leaf Church, my primary goal is to hear from God. I spend a good bit of my time praying, reading, thinking, dreaming, and writing. I am constantly asking God what he wants to do with his church in Cartersville.

Most big decisions and ministry initiatives in our church come from the Lead Team. This group is made up of three to five staff members who meet weekly. The Lead Team flies at 30,000 feet and discusses the overall ministry of the church. At our weekly meeting on Tuesday afternoon, we have a devotional time, evaluate Sunday's service, and talk through big picture items. We also approve any purchase requests that are over a certain dollar amount, and review the calendar.

Teamwork is one of our core values. During Lead Team meetings, we discuss everything—small groups, the worship service, the connections process, and more. In some churches, teamwork means that the senior pastor makes a decision and the rest of the staff works together to implement that plan. While I do reserve the right to make calls like that, it's very rare. Most of the time we discuss, debate and, decide things as a team.

However, teamwork does not mean that everyone gets an equal vote. It means that everyone gets an equal say. Our creative arts pastor might have some opinion about small groups, but in the end, our small groups pastor is responsible for managing and overseeing groups.

As the lead pastor, everyone knows that I can play the trump card. But I am very careful and sensitive with that responsibility. Leaders that come down from the mountain every couple of weeks with a new initiative or directive will be hard to follow. In our first couple of years as a church, I only played the trump card two times, and in both cases it was because I had a clear word from God.

Once a week, we have a one-hour all-staff meeting. Everyone that works at Oak Leaf Church—pastors, assistants, and interns attend this weekly meeting. I'll talk about vision and big picture things, making sure everyone is on the same page. We'll often read a book each month and discuss it during this meeting.

Our weekly all-staff meetings are the time when I share vision with the entire team. Sometimes we allow staff members to bring one of their key volunteers to this meeting, so they can be a part of the process. In addition to vision, each staff member gives an update on his or her ministry area. All-staff meetings help us stay on the same page.

If you'd like to see our staff organizational chart, visit *heretolead.com*.

Advisory Team

"A prudent person foresees danger and takes precautions. The simple one goes blindly on and suffers the consequences." –Proverbs 22:3

Though our bylaws do not call for a group like this, we believe that wise decisions are made with the advice of many counselors. So, I've put together a team of men who meet with me twice a month to provide wise counsel. This group looks at our financial statements and other reports. I ask them to report on the things that they see or hear in the church.

Since I don't see everything that happens in our church (any pastor that does is involved in way too many things), this group of people helps me foresee danger. I give them permission and freedom to talk to me about any area in our church. I intentionally don't have the staff in on these meetings in case they want to talk about the staff! It's a group of people who love Jesus and who love our church, and I value their opinions.

Here's the actual job description for those that serve on the advisory team.

Those who serve on the pastor's advisory team must:

1. Be an official member of Oak Leaf Church, having met all the criteria of membership.
2. Be a committed Christ-follower, servant of this church, and a leader for your family.
3. Be a regular giver. If you are not regularly contributing to the ministry of this church financially then your commitment isn't at the level appropriate to lead Oak Leaf Church in this way.
4. Be willing to provide honest feedback and wise counsel to the lead pastor. Our church and leaders need people who are comfortable saying what others won't.
5. Keep things in confidence. We need everyone who has access to sensitive information to have a confidentiality agreement on file and only discuss these things in these meetings.

This team will:

1. Meet about twice a month to provide insight and feedback to the lead pastor.
2. Review monthly financial statements. This team does not approve expenses, but in the spirit of honesty and accountability, takes a look at where we have been and where we are going.
3. Provide insight on key decisions.

This team will not:

1. Vote. Oak Leaf Church is a staff-led church. Our Board of Directors approves the budget. The Lead Team carries out the day-to-day ministry of the church. The pastor and staff are ultimately accountable for this ministry.
2. Be publicly recognized. Inclusion on this team should not be a matter of pride, because true leaders are servants.

Finance Team

As the lead pastor, I don't have my hand in the finances. I don't know the online banking passwords and I can't sign checks. I don't handle the offering or have access to the debit card.

I do have a credit card, and I get weekly updates on our financial situations, while the overall financial health of the church is my responsibility, I've chosen to work through our executive pastor in this area.

Our executive pastor meets with a finance team, who functions like his advisory team. Again, our bylaws do not *require* us to have a finance team, but we think it's a good idea. This team is made up of people who understand today's financial markets, who are good with their money, and who give to Oak Leaf Church. I would not put anyone on the finance team who does not contribute to our church. Jesus said their heart would follow their treasure, so if they aren't giving, then I'm not going to trust them to lead. In case you were still wondering, that means we do check giving records before we ask people serve in key leadership positions like this.

The finance team meets about once a month to review financial statements and look at projections.

To review, our bylaws describe the work of three groups of people. They are:

1. The Board of Directors
2. The Staff (including the lead pastor, the Lead Team and the staff)
3. The Membership

BUSINESS MEETINGS

Our bylaws say that we have one business meeting a year, to handle matters that are not "otherwise reserved for the staff." We could have more if they were necessary, but in general, we don't vote on things at Oak Leaf Church. We've created a culture that values participation, not attendance. We're not trying to create another political church, where a group of miscellaneous people in the church has the real power because of how they will vote in the upcoming business meetings. We don't even vote on our annual budget. Our staff prepares the budget, and the Board of Directors approves it. We talk about it and we make it available to people. We will answer every single question asked about it because we don't have anything to hide. But we don't need people overly involved in the administration of the church. We keep things lean and simple, so people can focus on ministry.

I don't really want to get involved in how my insurance company files our reports; I just want them to write me a check when my roof blows off my house. In the same way, I don't think most people care about the inner-workings of a church. They just want to know that we're on mission and leading with integrity.

FINANCIAL SYSTEMS

One of the most important places you need structure in your church is in the area of finances. As with most of our systems, we tried to create a system that would provide a certain level of accountability but still allow people flexibility and freedom to do their job.

Here are some of the highlights of our financial systems:

Approval

- Staff members can spend up to $100 without approval, provided the money has been allocated in their budget.
- Purchases that are more than $100 but less than $500 need the approval of the executive pastor.
- Purchases that are more than $500 need approval from the executive pastor and lead pastor.
- We will change these numbers as the size of our budget increases.

Receipts

- Every purchase must be documented with a receipt.
- Every staff member writes a budget code on the receipt so it is coded to the proper account.

- We turn in the itemized receipt, not just the credit card receipt.

Reimbursements

- The approval process applies to reimbursements.
- We don't give reimbursements for unauthorized expenses.
- There's an official reimbursement form.
- Nobody is reimbursed for a purchase that's more than thirty days old.

As the church grows, some of the numbers may change. But the principle behind them will remain the same. We are not trying to handicap ministry, but we do need to make sure that there is money in the bank. One of the toughest things for staff members that haven't been in ministry a long time to understand is this: just because it's in the budget doesn't mean it's in the bank.

TWO CAUTIONS

When it comes to systems, I want to give you two cautions. **First, don't install elders or put people in places of official leadership too soon**. It's wise to be light on systems (except for the financial systems), until there are some people that you know and trust. There will be people that come into your church plant from another church. They may have held a position of leadership at their former church and will offer to help. You'll be tempted to place them in positions of authority based on their experience, but this is a bad idea. You need to know their heart and get a good idea about their motive. You need to see them in action before giving them authority and the corresponding title.

I once invited a guy to be a part of my advisory team, even though I didn't know him well enough. He had come from another church and I wasn't patient enough. I was excited about getting him into leadership. A few months into it, I knew we were headed for trouble when he sat in my office and told me that he wanted to understand the why behind everything before he could support me publicly. I kindly told him that I needed people to support me publicly *no matter what*, and then come and talk to me. I walked into another staff member's office and predicted that he would leave our church within three months.

I was right, and he never even bothered to call and talk to me about his departure.

As Oak Leaf Church grows, we may go more toward some type of elder system. But as a brand new church, I didn't know these guys. If and when we install official elders, I want to see the fruit they produced over a number of years. I want to know that they are committed to the church, not to a title.

My second caution would be this: Don't try to please everyone. As you start the process of launching a church, you're going to meet people that were "burned by their last church" and want to talk about accountability. They want to know that you're not a dictator, and they are scared of labels like "staff-led." More often than not, these people are going to be disappointed in our system. We worked hard to create a system that balances accountability with trust, but I know it's not perfect. There is no perfect system.

Don't let critical or negative people have seats at the most important table. There is probably a reason that devil's advocate has the word devil in it. While there is a time and place for discussion, you can quickly identify if someone is working with the best interest of the church in mind.

SYSTEMS

In the first year, our church grew quickly—from a launch team of about twenty-five people to over eight hundred people on our one-year anniversary. A little after that one year mark, I had a mini-crisis, because I realized that we didn't have any systems in place to deal with the rapid growth. We had succeeded in getting people to church, but we hadn't answered the question, "What next?" How are we going to disciple these people? How are we going to stay organized?

We realized that we didn't have healthy systems to sustain this growth. You might not get excited about systems, and if you're a visionary church planter, systems might want to make you drive your car off a cliff. But systems are important.

If you're attracting people, but not keeping people, you could have a systems problem. If you're launching programs, and changing them all the time, that's a systems problem. Many of the problems we were facing were systems problems. We failed to realize that while systems were not sexy, they are a huge contributor to success. I was getting mad about problems in our church, but they would be repeated frequently because we were not addressing the systems that created the problems in the first place.

Eighteen months in, I went to work on our systems. I made a list of every system that needed to exist in our organization—things from how we hired and interviewed people, to how a service got planned, to how the truck was loaded. Next, we wrote them down.

Sometimes people aren't on the same page, because the actual page doesn't exist. It took us months and months and many meetings, but eventually, we wrote down every system in our church. We began to implement these systems, and do things the same way. It revolutionized the day-to-day operations of our church. People problems seemed to go away, because our people knew what we expected of them. Volunteers knew what they were responsible for and who to call in case they needed something. Meetings took shape because we knew the goal and the desired result.

When it comes to systems, the lead pastor may not be the best person to drive them. Most church planters are visionary leaders, who get drunk on vision. But somebody in your church is a systems thinker. Give them the reigns and ask them to go through your church looking for ways to make improvements. Give somebody a clipboard and ask them to observe setup and look for ways to speed it up.

Our lengthy systems analysis and corresponding documents eventually became Docs and Forms, a CD full of every document and form that we use at Oak Leaf Church. Church planters all across the country are taking these documents and customizing them for their environments. We're thrilled that we can save people hundreds of hours. If you're interested in Docs and Forms, you can get more information at *heretolead.com*.

CHAPTER 6:
BULLHORNS AND POSTCARDS

How are we going to get people to show up? That was a question I asked myself time and time again. Even now, I sometimes stand off to the side ten minutes before the first service and wonder if people are really going to show up.

I don't know of any church planter that didn't want a crowd of people at the first service. So much rides on that first service, and you want it to be successful.

In this chapter, I want to give you some of the specific practices that we used to spread the word and attract a crowd. But before we talk ideas, we need to lay some necessary philosophical groundwork.

There are many people that don't believe that advertising and Christianity should mix. I understand that sentiment, because there's a lot of lying in traditional advertising. Commercials on TV scream their message and try to attract customers. Our world has become so commercialized, so I completely understand how the church would want to push back from that.

Rob Bell is one of my favorite speakers in the world. I love his historical viewpoint and the way that he leads people on a journey through Scripture. When I listen to him teach, I want to dreidel or become a Rabbi.

Bell says, "The thought of the word church and the word marketing in the same sentence makes me sick."

Those are some strong words. In his first book, Rob Bell writes about the early days of his church plant. He says, "I remember being told that a sign had been rented with the church name on it to go in front of the building where we were meeting. I was mortified and had them get rid of it. You can't put a sign out front, I argued; people have to want to find us. And so there were no advertisements, no flyers, no promotions, and no signs." [7]

In 2005, Rob Bell went on a multi-city tour called "Everything is Spiritual." The tour has now been packaged into a DVD and is available from Zondervan. Here's the description of that product:

In the Hebrew Scriptures there is no word for spiritual. And Jesus never used the phrase spiritual life. Why? Because for Jesus and his tradition, all of life is spiritual.

During the tour, Rob Bell spends about twenty minutes talking about physics, including quantum mechanics. So here's my question. If everything is spiritual, can't advertising be spiritual? If God can speak to people through quantum mechanics, can't He also use a postcard?

Can advertising, marketing, and branding be used to advance the Kingdom of God? Rob Bell may be mortified at the thought of a sign at the entrance to his church, but can't God use a sign?

Let's take a look at Webster's definition of advertising.

Advertising- the act or practice of calling public attention to one's product, service, need, etc., esp. by paid announcements in newspapers and magazines, over radio or television, on billboards, etc.: to get more customers by advertising.

Advertising and marketing is simply calling attention to something. And isn't that something we want to do? Don't we want people to attend church? Don't we want the people in our community to meet Jesus? Don't we want to call people's attention to Jesus and His church?

---

[7] Velvet Elvis, page 99.

I don't think marketing is simply spiritual; I think it is *extremely* spiritual. Mark Batterson says over and over again, in bold phrases, "the greatest message ought to deserve the greatest marketing." I believe that marketing and advertising are outreach. Advertising can help you fulfill the great commission. Marketing can help you advance the Kingdom of God.

A church can grow without marketing, and God is certainly bigger than a marketing plan. There are many churches, in all parts of the world that grow without spending money on advertising. A good advertising campaign doesn't guarantee church growth or church health any more than a good sermon guarantees life change.

I don't think that a postcard will solve your problems, but marketing can be a useful tool in your arsenal.

GO AND TELL

When Andrew met Jesus in the Gospel of Mark, the first thing he did was go and tell his brother about his experience. When Jesus left the planet, he commissioned his disciples to go into all the world and make disciples. Over and over again, you see a "go and tell" message in the Bible. We are not supposed to sit back and wait for everyone to come to us. We are supposed to take the message of Jesus and his church to the people. The church is supposed to be missional, not just hold rallies and services and expect the world to come to us. We're supposed to go into the world, be salt and light, and tell people about our faith as we live life. The church needs to take the message to the people.

COME AND SEE

But there's another component to the message of Jesus. Throughout the New Testament, you read about great crowds. Jesus was somewhat of a celebrity, and there were people following him frequently. And over and over, Jesus looks at the crowd and has compassion on them. Jesus often withdrew from the crowds to pray, but he wasn't anti-crowd.

What did Andrew really do when He met Jesus? He went to tell his brother to come and see. As Christians, we're supposed to go and tell people to come and see. We're supposed to be missional *and* attractional.

Suzan is a lady in our church who heads up our prayer team. Every week, we receive prayer requests on our connection cards, and Suzan and her team faithfully lift these requests up to Jesus. I asked Suzan how she first found out about Oak Leaf Church and she told me, "All I know is I attended the preview services, was here on the first Sunday, and have been attending ever since because of a card that was sent in the mail."

Did advertising and marketing helped Suzan find her place of ministry in the Kingdom of God? Of course it did.

Let me ask it this way. Is someone that comes to your church via a personal invite less valuable than someone that comes to your church because of a postcard? Of course not.

Some people will say that we should simply preach the Gospel and leave the results to God. Some would say that marketing is a worldly method, and it should not be used.

Even if you would say that advertising and marketing are *worldly methods*, can't God redeem them for his purposes? We use science, history, and all sorts of worldly subjects in our church and in our church services. Language, psychology, and biology all help us understand humanity. Fairytales and references to pop culture teach us things about God. If God can use all these things – if everything really can be spiritual – then why limit God when it comes to marketing?

We survey our people all the time. In one of our surveys, we found that nearly 40 percent of our attenders came to Oak Leaf Church because of a postcard or a road sign. Only God knows if these people would have visited Oak Leaf Church by some other way, but I believe that God used our advertising campaigns. Personal invitations are the best, but marketing has helped people get connected to our church, where they have been challenged to go from where they are to where God wants them to be.

Mike Silliman[8], a church planter from West Grove, PA says, "I have found that personal invitations carry more weight and are more effective when supplemented with a mailer, yard sign, TV commercial,

---

[8] http://mikesilliman.blogspot.com/

or invite card. Jesus Christ through the local church is the hope of the world…I'm gonna use whatever creative resources that God has given us to bring people into our doors to experience life change!"

Marketing gives our people something to talk about. Sending out postcards helps our people extend personal invitations. When I invite people to our church, their first response is usually, "Yeah, I've heard of you guys." That happens because our people spread the word, but also because we're intentional about getting our name out there. Our marketing tools make it easier for people to invite their friends.

WHAT WORKS FOR US

Hopefully you want people to come to your church. And hopefully you understand that advertising *can* help you accomplish that. What kind of things work best? What do you do? How do you get the most bang for your buck? With the philosophical groundwork laid, let's dive into specifics.

As we started planning our preview services, we wanted to do everything we could to get people to attend. We had bought into this church, and we wanted everyone that didn't go to church somewhere to come to our church. We didn't have a lot of money, so we had to be creative and resourceful.[9]

Direct Mail

We lived in Cartersville for a year and a half before we held our first service. During that time, we only got one postcard from a church. And it really wasn't that good. Actually, it was pretty bad. I asked around and found out that churches really didn't use direct mail that much. At that moment, I decided that we would own the direct mail market in Cartersville.

We sent out five thousand postcards to announce our first preview service. We sent out ten thousand to announce our grand opening. We would have sent out more, but we didn't have enough money.

---

[9] Of all the sections in this book, this is the area where I feel that we act like motorboats instead of sailboats.

There are two ways to handle direct mail. One is easy and a little more expensive. The other is harder, but will save you some money.

Method #1: Use a mailing company.

After a lot of homework, we found a company that would take our design, print the postcards, and mail them for us. Their prices were great and their customer service was phenomenal. By far, this is the simplest way to get your message out via direct mail. You can mail to entire zip codes, specific postal routes, or to everyone within a certain radius of your meeting location. The company we use deals with the post office on our behalf. All we have to do is design the card. If you don't have a designer handy, they can even help you with the design.

Method #2: Saturation Mailout.

Work with the post office and do what they call a *saturation mailout.* Call the post office and find out how many routes there are in a particular zip code. You'll also find out how many boxes there are on each route. With this information, you'll distribute cards into mailing trays based on this information. The mail carrier will put a card in every box on his or her route. They are not individually addressed; you simply print "postal customer" on each card.

If you go this route, you'll save a little money because this is the cheapest postage rate. It will be extremely important to develop a good relationship with the person at the post office who handles bulk mail. You'll have questions about the paperwork, and having an ally at the post office will be a huge help. At the Cartersville Post Office, we've developed a great relationship with Tammy. We write her note cards and give her gift cards from time to time. She's helped us out of a jam on more than one occasion.

Surely, you want your postcard to stand out, get noticed, and result in first time guests coming to your church. When it comes to postcards there are several things that will make your project more effective.

MAKING THE MOST OF YOUR MAILOUTS

1. **Don't use stock cards from a stock company.** There are a lot of companies out there that will sell you prepackaged cards but I would advise against this. You need to design something that matches the look and feel of your church. Something personal, unique, and created by somebody that knows your church is always better than something generic created by professionals in another city. I actually learned how to use Adobe software and designed several of our postcards. A few months into our church, we began outsourcing our design work to designers who could do a better job. You don't consider your church a cookie-cutter church, so why use a cookie-cutter card to promote it?
2. **Send the larger postcards.** I would not send four by six postcard because they will just get lost in the shuffle. Spend the extra money to send the large cards, five and a half by eight and a half or larger. Remember, people get a lot of junk in their mailbox. Do your best to stand out.
3. **Make your cards interesting.** Nobody really cares to look at a church postcard with a picture of the building or a picture of the pastor. You've got to be more creative than that! Send something funny or something provocative. Send something that's going to get noticed. If you can't design a postcard with personality, save your money.
4. **Be different.** Mark Stevens says that whatever distinguishes your product should be the thing that is featured in your marketing. In other words, what is different about your church? What is unique about your service? Answer these questions and then design your postcard. I'm not sure that relevant teaching and contemporary music are all that different these days. You have to work hard to distinguish yourself.
5. **Avoid TMI.** Most of the church postcards I've seen have way too much information on them. You don't need to put your core values or your statement of beliefs on these things. Use a dominant picture and graphic and a simple title. Include your service times, a simple map, and your contact information. Make sure you include your phone number or website for

people who want more information. When you review the copy, go through and cut out every word that isn't absolutely necessary. ==Be ruthless about being simple.==

Direct mail works for us, but it may not work for you. If there are a bunch of churches in your area already utilizing direct mail, then you may want to find a different way to market your church. Or at least you'll have to do something that is dramatically different or far more noticeable. Direct mail is just one tool, and you need to use your knowledge of the area to determine if it will be effective.

We do three to five direct mail campaigns a year. Most of them will be tied to a series, since that typically generates the best response. I know of a few other churches in our area that will do campaigns the week before Easter, so although that will be our biggest day of the year, we're not going to do a direct mail. Instead, we're going to do one two weeks after Easter. If everyone is doing one thing, we like to do something different.

Several times a year, we'll also do a direct mail just to our database. If your church is like most, you probably have a ton of names and addresses in your database. It's much cheaper to mail to these people, and there's a good chance that most of them aren't coming to your church every week. We'll send them a direct mail tied to a new series to try to reengage them in our church.

Road Signs

==One of our most cost effective forms of advertising has been simple, corrugated plastic road signs that we put out on the weekend.==
In the summer of 2007, we put out road signs that simply said. "Boycott Oak Leaf Church. -Satan." We got the idea from LifeChurch.tv, who put that message on billboards. We put these signs around town and the phone started ringing. I think we printed the word "Satan" too small, because people called us nearly every day to tell us that someone had gone through a lot of trouble to print professional looking signs that talked bad about us. When we told them that we put those signs out, they still didn't understand.

That campaign turned out to be a little confusing to people, but as I thought about it, I realized that it was still good. My wife and I overheard several people talking about the campaign, trying to figure it out. I realized that if one person saw a message, they would read it and go about their day. If that message confused them, they might talk to someone about it, meaning that two people heard the message.

So I decided that if we can't make it clear, then we'd just try to confuse people.

Another road sign that we put out simply read "Chuck Norris [hearts] Oak Leaf Church." We put these signs all over town. We also printed the message on t-shirts and sold them at our resource table. The sign didn't have service times; we just put it out to be funny and to build buzz. People may not come to church directly because of that sign, but lots of people will talk.

We actually found a guy named Chuck Norris and asked him for permission to use his name. We sent him a gift card to say thanks. I have no idea where the real Chuck Norris lives, but the Charles Norris in Birmingham, Alabama really does love Oak Leaf Church.

In Buzzmarketing, Mark Hughes says that humor is one of the things that will create buzz. We've found that to be true.

We put out about fifty signs a weekend, and we lose about ten of them each week. At $3 or so each, that's a pretty good investment. Typically, we'll put the signs out for a month at a time, and then take a little break. If people get used to seeing something, they tune it out. (Which is why billboards may not be that effective for longer than a month or two.)

Approximately 18 percent of our people say they first came to Oak Leaf Church because they saw a road sign. That's a really big number, and these road signs are about the cheapest form of advertising we do.

Invite Cards

We print invite cards for every series we do. Three by three invite cards are so cheap to print. As we finish up a series, we always take a moment to remind our people that we're here to lead people from where they are to where God wants them to be. One way they can do that is by inviting people to church. We tell them that we're beginning a new series next week, and that it would be a great time to invite that unchurched person they know. Then, on the way out, our ushers give everyone three to four invite cards.

You can get creative with your invite cards. Elevation Church in Charlotte, North Carolina was doing a series build around eighties music and used cassette tapes as invites. We stole that idea when we did a similar-themed series. When we were gearing up to launch a Sunday night service in a bar, we printed invites on bar napkins.

Giving out invite cards is a great way to talk about inviting to your own people. Equip them with invite cards and challenge them to distribute them. Challenge people to give them to people in the drive-thru. Ask business leaders to display them in their stores and shops. Wherever people put out business cards, leave a stack of invites. Don't just provide invite cards for your people; show them how to use them.

In 2010, once we were in a permanent facility, we built a very large display near the exit of our auditorium. This display is stocked with all sorts of invite cards—from series specific invites to Saturday night services to kids events. Not only do our people take them and pass them out on a regular basis, the display itself is a constant reminder to our people that we value inviting.

Community Outreach Events

Some of the most effective marketing happens when you decide to be a presence in the community. I am convinced that our church should be known in the community. I tell our people all the time that one of my core convictions is that people should miss us if we went away. We ought to make life better for everyone in Cartersville, even if they don't go to our church. Maybe *especially* if they don't go to our church.

When we started Oak Leaf Church, we made a conscious decision to be at as many community events as we could. One of the first things we did was setup a moonwalk at a downtown car show. During the summer, our city does car shows once a month on the square, and hundreds of people come out to walk around. We offered to setup the moonwalk and it gave us the chance to talk to hundreds of people. We let their kids jump in the moonwalk for free and we handed out invite cards.

There's a big festival on the 4th of July in one of our local parks. Before we even launched, we had a presence at this event. Most vendors sell food or crafts, but we just setup the moonwalk and gave away helium balloons. Since most people charged money for things, we really stood out. Not to mention the fact that we were the only church there. Once again, we were able to add value to an event in our community, and meet hundreds of people. That first July, we met a guy named Keelan. We gave him an invite card and he came to our grand opening service. About a year later, I performed his wedding ceremony. Keelan is now part of our production team and runs lights; his wife, Mache is our bookkeeper.

On Halloween night, many of the downtown shops give out candy and the night has turned into quite an event. Thousands of families come out to trick or treat, so we knew we wanted to be a part of that event. A lot of the churches in our area organize some kind of fall festival, but we didn't want to separate ourselves from the community, we wanted to get right in the middle of it. We gave away candy (good candy, not that orange and black mystery stuff) and helium balloons. Seeing hundreds of children walk around with red balloons sporting our logo and website was quite a sight. In fact, the balloons were more popular than the candy.

We gave out more than two thousand invite cards that night, and we were the only church there. Now, there are a bunch of other churches that have followed suit.

Some churches choose to boycott the "devil's holiday"; other churches decide to create an alternative experience. We choose to leverage the day to invite people to church.

Instead of creating your own outreach event, consider teaming up with something that already happens in your city or county. Since there are so many churches that do fall festivals in our area, we decided that it wouldn't be an effective use of money to add another one to the mix. However, there are lots of elementary schools that do fall festivals every year. Instead of doing your own, why not call up the school and offer to make theirs better?

In 2008, we decided to sponsor a "teacher of the month gift" for one of our local schools. We found out that the teacher of the month didn't even get a certificate, so we decided to jump in and help. We gave the teacher of the month a gift card to Longhorn Steakhouse.

Every now and then we show up at a local school or business with a bunch of sausage biscuits. We say "thanks" or "good job" and leave biscuits and coffee for breakfast. We don't do it for the recognition; we do it because it's nice.

I love hearing stories of how other churches serve their community. Jeff Kapusta, a church planter in Tennessee told me about their free gas giveaway. JR Lee partnered with Wal-Mart to challenge people to purchase bikes for underprivileged children. I know of a church that hosted a poker tournament to raise money for a child advocate program.

All of these projects helped spread the word about a church, but more importantly, they met needs in the community. I think the church should be on the forefront of community service.

No bank, civic group, or non-profit organization should outshine the church when it comes to serving the community.

TRACK THE RESULTS

Good marketers will advise you to track the results of your efforts. In fact, Mark Stevens, author of *Your Marketing Sucks,* says that you should immediately stop all marketing unless you can measure effectiveness. In other words, if you don't know that people are coming to your church because of a postcard, then you're wasting money. Stevens says that name recognition is a concept invented by marketers to justify the massive amounts of money being spent. I'd tend to agree. After all, I don't just want people to know that Oak Leaf Church exists; I want them to actually attend.

A survey is a great way to track your results. In addition to periodic surveys through Constant Contact, we put a small survey on the connection card that first time guests fill out on the weekends. We ask guests to let us know how they heard about us. Each week, we learn that people come because of a postcard, a road sign or because of the invitation of a friend.

We ask them to write the name of the friend that invited them, and I'll often send that person a thank you note. I'll thank them for partnering with us and helping us advance the mission of Jesus in Cartersville and include a $5 Starbucks gift card. I want to thank the guest for giving our church a try, but I also want to thank and encourage the person that invited them.

If you notice that a particular form of advertising isn't working, then it's time to change things up. Don't just do things that worked in the past; do things that work now. God may want to do something new. If you don't know that people are coming to your church because of postcards, then you might be spending a lot of money for nothing.

ADVERTISING ON A BUDGET

Like most churches, we didn't have money when we started. Come to think of it, we still don't. We have to be selective, and we have to work on a budget.

We do always work to increase that budget, because we know that so much begins with getting people to church on the weekend. In many ways, it's a catch-22. You don't have enough people on the weekend to generate the revenue to do advertising, but since you can't do advertising, you won't get more people there on the weekend. It might be time to make a tough decision to say no to something else, so you'll have money available for outreach and marketing.

Think of companies like McDonald's and Coca-Cola. If anyone could get by on name recognition or word-of-mouth, it would be huge companies like this. But they spend millions on advertising, and are constantly increasing their marketing budgets.

I wish we had money in the budget to fund every advertising campaign or outreach event that we've dreamed up, but we don't. We have to cut some corners and we have to be smart. Here are some ways you can market on a budget.

1. **Find freelance designers.** You don't have to have a full-time graphic designer on your staff to create compelling pieces. Investigate local colleges or even high school graphic design classes. In many times, there are students who would be happy to do work on the side.
2. Check out full color **online printers.** I do believe there is a value in doing business locally, but it's hard to compete with the big online printers when it comes to cost. You can get one thousand full color business cards for $29. You can get twenty-five hundred full color postcards for $200.
3. For one series, which was during a time when money was really tight, we printed postcards and gave them to our people and asked them to address and mail them. We joked with them

that they could invite a friend or neighbor without even talking to them.

If you ask God for ideas, He will give them to you. If you look for ways to spread the word and advance the Kingdom, you'll find them. Remember, the church belongs to God. He wants people there even more than you do.

CHAPTER 7:
WHAT WE WANT TO DO WELL, PART ONE

As a church planter with three young children, it's tough to go out to dinner with my wife. Those nights out without the kids are hard to plan and hard to finance. Dinner, a movie, and a babysitter starts to push $100. This is largely due to the fact that I just can't go to a movie without ordering a large popcorn and a 72-ounce coke.

In January of 2008, my wife and I reorganized our weekly date night into something that is lighter on the budget and easier on the schedule. One night a week, we put the kids to bed as usual. Once they are asleep, we cook dinner together. It makes for a late dinner by the time it's finished, but we both enjoy cooking, so it's a great way for us to spend time together. And hey, it makes dessert all the more interesting if you know what I mean.

I'm no chef, but there are a couple of standards when it comes to preparing a good meal. In fact, the quality of the meal can be directly related to the proper ingredients and the proper conditions.

On our date night, I'll usually go to the store and pick up the things that we need. I'm careful to get the right items, because there's a big difference between curry and cumin.

You need the right ingredients to make a good dinner. I think starting a church is much like that. You must have the right ingredients.

Too many ingredients can mess up a dish. Throwing the wrong ingredient in the mixing bowl may ruin it.

To create a good meal, you also need the right conditions. The oven, stove or grill needs to be set at the right temperature, depending on the recipe. As a church planter, you'll work hard to create the right environment. Just like the temperature of the oven needs to be set correctly, you need to keep an eye on the thermostat of your church. It's easy to drift a few degrees and run the risk of messing up the meal.

Our goal on the weekend is to create an environment where God is most likely to work.

MAKING SUNDAY BETTER

Bill Clinton got elected to the White House in the nineties by focusing on the economy. One of his famous statements was, "It's the economy, stupid." That simple statement allowed him to focus on the issues that he believed mattered most to Americans. Sure, there were lots of other issues that needed attention, but he believed this issue was the most relevant for citizens.

If Clinton's major focus was the economy, then I believe the focus of a church planter ought to be the weekend. There are a ton of other important issues – leadership development, student ministry, small groups, etcetera, but I believe all of those issues can flow from what happens on the weekend.

For us, the weekend is the front door. This is especially true during the first few months of a church. It's really not rocket science: if you have a good weekend experience, people will probably come back. And if they come back, there is a good chance that they will connect to a volunteer team, join a small group, or start reading their Bible.

If guests are turned off by something that happens on the weekend, they won't take another step. For that reason, I believe church planters and everyone in leadership positions at a new church should focus the majority of their energy on the weekend experience.

Systems are great, but if people don't connect on the weekend, then those systems aren't going to matter!

As I was running on the treadmill one afternoon, I watched two guys ride up to the outdoor basketball court in my neighborhood. I watched one of the guys practice half-court shots almost exclusively. Now, the half-court shot, when made, is pretty exciting. There have even been games won with a half-court shot. But for the most part, these shots aren't an important part of the game. Basketball games are won with defense, lay-ups, easy shots, and open jumpers. The half-court shot may be sexy, but it's not important. The player that could make 50 percent of them at the *end* of the game but couldn't play defense the *entire* game wouldn't be much help to the team.

In life, business, and especially ministry, we need to excel at the little things and not put so much hope in the long shot. It's our successful lay-ups or free-throw shots that are going to make us successful. How much practice do we devote to the sexy things, while letting the everyday or every week things just run themselves? In reality, the daily or weekly things affect more of the bottom line.

It's the free-throw shots and lay-ups, not the half-court shots that matter most.

One of our "best practices" at Oak Leaf Church keeps us from practicing things that don't matter. We don't want to do anything that would take away from the weekend services. That means that we don't allow small groups to meet on Sunday morning. We don't do high school ministry during the weekend services since that would take volunteers away from the environment that matters most. We limit the amount of things that happen right after the service, since people can't bring their friends to church with them if they have to stay after the service for some meeting. We are already competing with the lake, IHOP, and cleaning out the garage—we don't want to compete with some other church ministry. We want the services to be *the* focus of the weekend.

One reason that we keep the weekend simple is that we challenge our church to bring their friends. If our regular attenders have two or three things to do before or after the services, they aren't likely to bring a friend to church.

Every church plant cuts corners, but don't cut corners when it comes to the weekend. Don't skimp out on the things that people will see. Get a cheaper office printer, or get rid of the entire office before you cut things that are visible on the weekend. We will sell all the computers in the office and track expenses on an abacus before we get rid of signs in our lobby. The things that are seen by the most people should be the last things that are cut.

All of our staff, from the bookkeeper to the executive pastor, have responsibilities on the weekend. Our connections pastor serves as a greeter. Our executive pastor works with kids check-in. These ministries happen on the weekend, and that's our bread and butter.

In *Good to Great*, Jim Collins talks about focusing on what drives your economic engine. In other words, put your focus on the things that matter most. For us, all other ministries in the church depend on the success of the weekend.

In the early months of our church plant, we put nearly 100 percent of our energy into the weekend. We knew that we wanted to attract a crowd to the movie theater, where we held our services. We've never set one attendance goal, but in my head, I knew that two hundred people attending a new church would generate a lot of buzz. I prayed for people to show up to that first service, and I still pray for people to show up on the weekends. The amount of time that our staff spends getting ready for Sunday is still pretty high. We devote a ton of time and energy to this every week.

One of the most important things you can do as a church planter is to get ready for the weekend. I know you have things pulling you in all different directions, but are you doing the weekend services to the best of your ability? Do you need to spend more time on your message or improving the environment? Do you need to say no to something so you can focus on Sunday?

When we launched the church, I got to the theater at 6:00 a.m. with the rest of our setup team. I wanted to get there early so I could teach our volunteers how we should do things. Looking back on this time, I was forging and refining our best practices while on the job. I would walk around the lobby and rearrange things, and in the process, talk with our volunteers about excellence. I would go over to the kid's check-in table and talk about how more sheets of paper on the table actually took away from the clear communication of information. I would help the ladies at the product table organize t-shirts in a more appealing way. I would grab a volunteer and show them why an empty plastic bin had to be moved down the hall and be out of sight.

I would personally evaluate the size of the font on the screen and rearrange the stage to make things simpler. I'm sure people thought I was OCD or ADD, or some kind of weird combination of the two.

I don't do this as much anymore, because our best practices are filtering their way through our culture. People understood the why and they began to make decisions based on the same guiding principles. But it started with a commitment on my part to do everything I could to make the weekend the best it could be.

TEACHING

==As a church planter, preparing your message has to be your top priority.== Sadly, I think most church planters don't spend enough time on their message. It's understandable, because in addition to teaching on the weekend, you've also got to create the handout, update the website, meet with the greeters, balance the budget, organize the community outreach event, meet with people in the community, and answer people's questions about the church. It's a rough schedule, and the first six months can be brutal.

==But you have to find a way to elevate message preparation to the top of that list.== If people do not hear from God during our services, then you're just spinning your wheels. I don't go to yahoosermons.com and download a message on Saturday night; I work really hard, weeks and months in advance on messages.

I want to challenge you to hear from God when it comes to your teaching. There are some amazing teachers out there, but that doesn't mean you need to preach their sermons. I'll listen to other messages for inspiration and I borrow material all the time. But I don't download messages from the Internet and teach them word for word. I don't do that because I have something to say. God has given me a message, and I want to tell people. It's time for us to start teaching our people because God has given us a message, not because Ed Young just finished a series.

No matter how cutting edge your music is, no matter how many fancy videos you produce, and no matter how fun your children's environments are, people will continue to attend your church because they hear a message that challenges them. Lame sermons just don't cut it.

You have to hear from God, the one who puts the wind in the sails of the church. Remember, you're building a sailboat, not a motorboat.

A TEACHING CALENDAR

The thing that helps me stay on top of things is developing a teaching calendar. I know there are guys who like to pray on Monday and hope the Holy Spirit speaks to them by Friday, but I like to give God more time than that. The same spirit that spoke to Moses from a burning bush can speak to me when Microsoft Excel is open on my computer screen.

At the beginning of the year, we go through a process of laying out the teaching calendar. As we plan things out, I ask three questions.

- What does God want me to say? I think this is the key. There are too many pastors teaching on something because they found a cool graphic on the Internet or their favorite celebrity teacher just finished with it.
- What does our staff think we need to talk about? We go away for a day or two on a sermon planning retreat. Our goal for that retreat is to answer the question, "What Does God want the people at Oak Leaf Church to hear this year?" Then we organize those ideas into a teaching calendar.
- What do our people want to know? Once or twice a year, we survey our people and ask them what they want to know. Last year, I was surprised that so many people wanted to know about angels and demons. That information helped us plan a three-part series on the subject. The book of 1 Corinthians in the New Testament was written to answer questions that the church asked Paul. In much the same way, I think we should teach on things that our people want to hear.[10]

Having a teaching calendar will allow you to prepare months in advance for messages. If you know you are teaching on family in the

---

[10] We've used constantcontact.com to do surveys, and we also do impromptu surveys on the weekends using text messages.

fall, then when you see a news article or read a blog entry, you can save it and come back to it later. If your staff knows where you're going, then they can do the same thing.

I change the teaching calendar all the time, moving messages to different times of the year. And we've been known to call an "audible" from time to time because of how God leads. But the teaching calendar helps us in so many ways, including:

- Our creative people know where we're going so they can choose and practice songs that fit the theme.
- We have time to make or find videos.
- Because we're ahead a few weeks, we can change things up if God says to go in a different direction.
- We can save money on props and printing, because we don't have to rush jobs.
- We don't stress our graphics guys out with questions like, "I know it's Thursday, but can I get a picture of a guy in a cheerleading outfit skydiving out of a submarine."

You can see a sample of our teaching calendar at *heretolead.com*. By the way, we also make most of our message notes and graphics available for free as well. This stuff shouldn't substitute you hearing from God, but maybe it can jumpstart your thinking or supplement your study.

DO YOUR HOMEWORK

I typically prepare for messages a few weeks in advance. Since we've worked hard to lay out the teaching calendar, I know where we're going. When it comes time to start serious preparation, I usually have some content.

Some people block out entire days to study and write. I'm a little ADD so I can't work that way. Two hours of reading is a long time for me. I can't sit still—I bite my fingernails, and my mind is always in three places at once. I should have probably been on multiple medications as a child. It's always been tough for me to have a quiet time, because I'll start out reading in Genesis and end up flipping through Time magazine.

Part of me wishes I could just block off an entire day of the week for study time, but I can't work that way. I'd rather devote one hour here and one hour there. Planning out far in advance actually allows me to work on several messages at a time, and it allows me to work within my rhythm.

I block out a few hours on Monday, a few hours on Thursday, and I actually do some of my best work on Sunday night. That's the rhythm that works for me. <u>You have to find your rhythm and stick to it</u>. It's important to carve out adequate time to study, pray, and work on your messages. If you don't make it a priority, something will always snatch your time away.

A few months ago, I also changed my schedule up a bit. I moved Monday's staff meeting to Tuesday and now I don't do any meetings on Monday. Instead, I use that time to reflect on the previous weekend and finish my message for the upcoming weekend. It's my most important task of the week, so I want to get it done early. It's kind of like giving—<u>I want to give sermon preparation my first chunk of time and not my leftovers</u>. I also do most of my meetings in the afternoon, since I'm usually the most productive in the morning. I use those morning hours to study and prepare for meetings.

A side benefit of this schedule change is that our production people have the final version of my message five days in advance. I'm also able to schedule meetings and get other things done knowing that my message is ready to roll.

GET HELP

<u>On Tuesday mornings we have a creative meeting.</u> In addition to reviewing the program order for the coming week, we go through a message that will be delivered in a few weeks. I bring a message that is nearly complete and ask for feedback and ideas. I ask them what should be cut and what should be expanded. They chime in with stories or video ideas. Since we're talking about a message that is usually three weeks away, we have time to make changes and make things better. Sometimes the sermon meeting happens several weeks before I write the message. I ask people to bring ideas, points, and illustrations on a particular topic, and we study a passage together.

Early on, this was a monthly meeting fueled by volunteers. We didn't have a staff, so I gathered together about ten people in our church and we talked through an entire series. I asked them for creative ideas and input on content. Some great ideas came out of those meetings. If you don't have a large staff, consider inviting some volunteers to join you once a month to fuel your creative planning.

If you don't have a team of volunteers, consider sending your finished message to another pastor. Ask him for feedback and advice, and then don't be too prideful to listen.

SAY IT WITH PICTURES

We work hard to come up with memorable ways to help people connect with God's truth. You know from personal experience that people don't remember sermons. If I gave you fifteen minutes to write down information from all the sermons you've heard, you'd probably struggle to fill up one sheet of paper. And if that would be true for you, a church leader, imagine how much more true it would be for the average Joes or Janes in your church.

We don't have to make the Bible relevant, it already is. But in today's culture, we have to fight to make the Bible memorable. I want people to remember spiritual truths at work or at school, and that's tough.

We never start with the illustrations; we always start with God's Word and the principles found there. But I've learned that memorable illustrations can help people remember.

Jesus reinforced his identity with miracles. These dramatic events were illustrations that showed people that he really was the Son of God. In his teaching, he frequently used parables. Some didn't get the point of these stories with a purpose, so he would later explain them to his followers. Jesus also used examples from fishing and farming to help illustrate his points to the listeners.

Since I can't walk on water or multiply bread, I have to use stories and illustrations to illustrate and explain God's Word. We constantly look for over-the-top illustrations or driving metaphors that will help people remember God's Word. Here are three sermon illustrations I've used in the past:

1. In order to help people realize that we should be offensive, not defensive, we built a bunker on the stage. During the message, I walked over to the bunker, put on a camouflage jacket and helmet and picked up a pellet gun. I talked about how most Christians want to hunker down in the bunker to keep themselves safe from the world. However, Jesus said the gates of hell would not prevail against the church—that's a picture of offense. When I looked up from that bunker, I saw five or six people taking pictures with their cell phones. I'd say it's a win if people are taking pictures in church so they can tell their friends.[11]

2. During a message on sex, I setup a small kitchen island on the stage. Throughout the sermon, I referred to things on the table. At one point, I compared the world's view of sex to a meal eaten on a paper plate. They use it up and throw it away when they are finished. God wants us to treat sex more like fine china. When we deviate from God's plan, we smash the plate. I threw the plate down on the stage and glass went everywhere. I love breaking things in church, because it's memorable. Hopefully, people will remember that illustration.

3. During a message on small groups, we used a three-legged table to illustrate how our lives operate. One leg represented our inside life – our character and beliefs. One leg represented our activities – our job or hobbies. The third leg represented our relationships. I told people that small groups were the only place in our church where all three of these come together. By refusing to mix your personal life with your relationships, you're setting yourself up for long-term failure. Then, I whipped out a chain saw and sawed off one of the legs and talked about how a two-legged table won't stand up.

Creativity is hard work, and it's tough for me to come up with ideas like that. That's why I value our Tuesday morning creative meetings.

WHAT DO WE WANT PEOPLE TO KNOW?

Fueled by the belief that some truths about Christianity are so foundational, we developed a list of five key principles that we really

---

[11] Watch these and other videos from our church on youtube.com and vimeo.com. You'll find links at oakleafchurch.com.

want people to know. Throughout the year, we teach about these truths in different ways. I keep these principles on my desk and come back to them time and time again.

- <u>People matter to God.</u> When you serve others by putting them first, you'll experience joy.
- <u>You can't earn the favor of God.</u> When you understand grace and live by grace, you'll experience freedom.
- <u>You can trust God with your life.</u> When you understand the character of God, you'll experience true peace.
- <u>Life is not meant to be lived alone.</u> When you live in community and develop authentic relationships, you'll experience true fellowship.
- <u>Make wise decisions.</u> When you see God as the source of wisdom and apply his principles to your life, you'll experience positive results.

These guiding principles drive my teaching. I could speak at will, with little preparation on any of these topics.

WORSHIP

The second thing that we want to do well on the weekend is worship.

When we started the church, we did not have a worship leader on staff. But I also knew that we needed to have excellent music from day one. Since the weekend was the event that people would use to judge our young church, we had to have quality music. A guy with an acoustic guitar singing James Taylor versions of Passion songs wasn't going to cut it.

So, we hired bands and pretended that they were our own. We got better quality, and it was actually cheaper than hiring a full-time worship pastor. <u>We got a whole band for the cost of one guy</u>.

As I said earlier in the book, we had Tenth Avenue North lead worship for us a few times. We also used other local bands for the first three months of our church. This turned out to be a great experience for us, because it allowed us to have quality music from the beginning. <u>Good music attracted good musicians,</u> and after about six months, we found out that we had some great players and singers attending our church.

One of the guys that we brought in to lead was Will Goodwin. He and his band did a great job, so we invited them back. He and his wife even came to our church a few times when he wasn't leading. Nine months into it, we asked Will to lead for us on a more regular basis. In January of 2008, he joined our staff as our full-time creative arts pastor.

⌈ The strategy of bringing in bands for the first few months turned out to be one of the best decisions we ever made. ⌉

PAYING MUSICIANS

We don't have a problem with paying musicians to play, but we'd rather have people that are committed to our church, who play because they want to use their gifts, not because they want a paycheck.

I am not a huge fan of the worship musician culture that I see in Atlanta—gifted and talented musicians going to play at whatever church pays the best.

The guys and girls that play at Oak Leaf Church care about our church. They arrive early to setup their equipment, and they stay after the service to help tear down the stage and sound system. They aren't just playing because they like being on stage; they are playing because they love Jesus and love the church.

Most churches that pay musicians argue that these musicians make their living by playing. It's not a hobby; it's their way of life. I do understand this, but we have full-time schoolteachers working in our children's environments. We have IT professionals working with computers. They have been educated and trained in their field, so should we pay them as well? The people that play in the band work hard, and put a lot of time into making the weekend services sound great, but we also have setup guys that work for six hours every Sunday. Doesn't the Bible teach that all the parts of the body are important? I believe part of discipleship is developing someone's gifts to build up the body of Christ.

There is no right or wrong when it comes to paying musicians. You have to do what fits your culture and what fits your long-term plan.

CHAPTER 8:
WHAT WE WANT TO DO WELL, PART TWO

I believe that the weekend is the most important thing we do as a church. It's important to have systems in place, but those systems must lead to a strong weekend.

CHILDREN AND STUDENTS

The third point of emphasis in our church is children and student ministries. Study after study show that most people become Christians before they reach their eighteenth birthday.

On any given weekend, about 28 percent of the total attendance at Oak Leaf Church is children. Therefore, providing quality and meaningful programming for children is one of the most important things we do on the weekend.

Along with teaching, it's why people will stay at your church. They may come because a friend invited them or because they got a postcard in the mail, but they will stay because they are growing closer to God and because their children are learning about God as well. Over and over again, we hear from people in our community that the reason they decided to get back into church was because of their kids.

In addition to being a pastor, I'm also the father of three pretty important kids. I know firsthand how important it is for children to learn about God in a fun and engaging way. I'm thrilled that there are other people speaking truth into my children's lives.

Having quality children's environments is so important to me that I've attended children's ministry conferences. I don't think we should just leave next generation ministries to other people on staff; I want to be a vital part. Our children's ministry and student ministry staff will always know that they have my support. I will push for their budgets to be increased every year.

CHILDREN'S MINISTRY IN PORTABLE ENVIRONMENTS

When we were in launch team mode, we put our best people in our children's environment. One of those people became our first part-time children's ministry leader. She worked so hard in those early months to make sure things were covered, and within a matter of months, there were more than one hundred children attending Oak Leaf Church each week.

In those first few months, money was so tight that we couldn't afford to rent multiple rooms in the movie theater. We borrowed portable walls from another church, and divided the hallways into kid's classrooms. It wasn't an ideal situation, but we made the best of it. When we were financially able, we moved into additional theaters.

Members of our launch team went to garage sales and consignment sales to find cribs, changing tables, toys, and baby swings. We outfitted much of our kid's areas from those garage sales. Even though we didn't have much money, we maintained an attitude of excellence. Is it possible to do great things on a budget when you have the right attitude? Yes!

When we moved into additional theaters, we were able to ramp up the production of our elementary program. We added a sound system, lights and some props to create an environment called the City.

Elementary children absolutely loved coming to a movie theater for church.

It's tough to create warm and friendly nursery environments in a twelve-foot-deep space at the front of a movie theater, but a few simple things really helped:

- We used pipe and drape to create a backdrop. We printed full color, billboard-size graphics to add some color to the room. We made the rooms looks great.
- We used two-foot by two-foot foam squares to cover the floor. It brightens things up and it's much cleaner than the movie theater floor.
- Since lights were always out in the theater, we brought in shop lights to add even more light. <u>Overcoming the dark feel of the theater was one of our most important priorities</u>. This was one of the toughest things to overcome in the movie theater setting.

We made sure our kids hallways were safe and secure, having a check-in system from day one. We used two-part stickers in the beginning, but have since moved to a computer-based system.

We made sure we had identifiable security guards that were visible to parents.

One of the best purchases we ever made for our kid's environments were portable, rolling cases from Portable Church Industries. We didn't have money to buy them new (do you sense a theme?), but we found some used at a church in another state. We made a two-day road trip and saved about $1,500. We were able to get a giant case for each classroom, and it made setup go so much smoother.

CURRICULUM

We used a DVD-based curriculum called KidMo, and showed the teaching elements on the big screen. From time to time, we'd bring in someone to do live music. After the teaching element, the children would break up into small groups. They would just sit right there on the floor as a leader would guide them through a discussion.

Feeling like we could do a little better, we switched to what I believe is the most comprehensive children's ministry curriculum out there—252 Basics. We loved the format and the underlying principles, but it was just too volunteer intensive for us, as a portable church.

We settled on something in between—Elevate, which is put out by CreativePastors and Fellowship Church. It's fun, series-based and easy to use. It really helped take our elementary environment to the next level.

In the preschool environments, we use First Look. As we've experimented with different curriculum, we've come to realize that the quality of our ministry is more directly related to the quality of our people than the quality of the material. Just like there are schools that have the latest and most accurate books, churches can have the latest and greatest resources. But implementation is the task that falls to your people. A good teacher and a committed leader can do a lot with a little.

My challenge to you would be to focus your time and energy on developing your people, not searching for the perfect curriculum.

One of the reasons that we quickly moved to two services was our Oak Leaf Kids volunteers. Like most churches, we had some committed people that rarely got to attend the church service. We rotated them in and out, and that worked okay for a few months.

When we went to two services, we got rid of all rotations. This was huge! It simplified so many things. Our volunteers serve during one service and attend the other.

STUDENTS

It's possible to put a great emphasis on student ministry without creating a bunch of programs that will just busy up the calendar. The student ministry at Oak Leaf Church is pretty simple, and I'm sure there are parents that don't think we are doing enough. But we're not trying to keep teenagers busy; we're trying to help them become disciples. We aren't trying to entertain teenagers; we're trying to help them follow Jesus.

First of all, our student ministry is built on the fact that teenagers can be full-fledged disciples. They are not mini-Christians or disciples in training. 1 Timothy 4:12 says that teenagers are to be examples to the whole church in a variety of spiritual disciplines. We believe the goal of student ministry is to disciple students, in the same way we disciple adults. We are not trying to busy up the lives of teenagers with bowling nights, weekend events every other weekend, and $600 camps and retreats.

We want students to be a part of the church. I am absolutely convinced that the main reason teenagers leave the church after high school is because they were never part of the church in the first place. They were part of an event-driven youth group, but they were never part of the church. So…

CHURCH IS FOR TEENAGERS

We design our weekend services with students in mind. Middle school and high school students can and should attend church. It's appropriate for them, and they will learn something about God. They will like the music and the messages and they won't be bored. I often speak directly to them from the stage and I'll drop cultural references in my messages that I know they will get.

Before you rush out and start a weekly youth group service, ask yourself why teenagers need another service. If you're like most church plants, you have one service on Sunday morning for adults. Why do teenagers have twice as many church services as adults?

We challenge students to bring their friends to church. Now there's a novel idea! Instead of pushing students to bring their friends to bowling nights, weekend events, pillow fights and Disney World trips, we ask them to bring their friends to church. That's the same exact thing we do for adults. We want everyone in our church to bring people they know.

LET STUDENTS VOLUNTEER

Nearly every volunteer opportunity in our church is open to teenagers. Frankly, there should be *many more* teenagers serving in our church. They need to use their gifts and abilities (and they have many) in the body of Christ, in which they are a vital part.

Teenagers should be greeting people, working with children, doing drama and singing in elementary environments, working with computers, directing traffic, and I could go on. When students get on these teams, they are getting around adults who love Jesus and they will be part of a multi-generational team. That's a good thing.

Sadly, there are too many volunteer areas that are off-limits for teenagers at a lot of churches. There might be dozens of teenagers that are capable of running computers and helping with technology. In fact, teenagers might be more qualified because they have grown up with computers. I worked in a church where the sound room was effectively off limits to teenagers. The church didn't trust them with the expensive equipment. But over in our student facility, we were doing things better and students ran it all. Instead of keeping teenagers working with students, we should have utilized their gifts and abilities in the church.

Middle school students can serve in certain environments in our kid's areas. High school students can work with preschool and elementary children. Teenagers can help check-in children or help park cars. They can be ushers and greeters. They can come early and setup or stay late to tear down. Nearly every volunteer position in our church is open to teenagers.

I believe that high school students leave the church after graduation because they were never involved in the church in the first place. Sure, there are teenagers who come to youth services or sign up for youth camp, but never connect with the church. They are committed to their youth group, but they aren't committed to the church.

It's time to turn the tide. We need to stop treating student ministry like an activity club and go all out to connect teenagers to the overall mission of the church.

SPECIAL EVENTS

We do plan some special events, but we are not an event-driven student ministry. We didn't hire a student pastor to baby-sit teenagers and make sure that their calendar is full. We hired a student pastor to reach students, involve them in our church, help them connect with a small group, and help them find a place to use their gifts in the church.

When I think about the many event-driven youth groups that I've worked with over the years, I wonder how successful all those events are at accomplishing the bottom line mission. How many youth pastors fill their schedules with planning lock-ins and bowling nights when they could be developing leaders or making disciples?

DON'T START A YOUTH GROUP

One of the mistakes we made during our first six months, was we tried to launch a traditional youth group. It's odd to me, because I was a youth pastor for a dozen years. You'd think I would be good at launching a youth group.

Since our church was new and exciting, we attracted a bunch of families that had teenagers. Our original plan was to wait one year before putting any effort into student ministry. But three months into our church, we looked around and realized that there were dozens of teenagers coming to church. We got trigger happy, and we moved too fast.

We hired a part-time youth pastor and launched a Thursday night youth service. We rented a room off-site, printed some t-shirts, and launched a youth service with about eighty people. For perspective, that was probably the third largest youth group in our county.

Over the next few months, it dwindled down to twenty people. It was inconsistent. The music wasn't as good as the music we had in our weekend service. We weren't able to put a great communicator on the stage. The night we pulled the plug, there were about ten people there.

Throughout the next few months, we struggled with what to do. Parents kept asking what we were going to do for students. We tried to plan a few events, but there wasn't much interest. It was very frustrating.

We moved our youth ministry meeting to once a month on Sunday morning. Since students were already there, we decided to keep something going. Even though we'd have seventy-five teenagers there, most of them preferred attending our regular service. Eventually, we came to the conclusion that we did not need to offer a traditional student ministry. Nathan, our student pastor decided to focus on small groups, getting students serving within the church, and organizing a monthly outreach service. After lots of trial and error, I felt we were finally clicking with our student environments, mainly because we decided to be simple.

If I could go back and do it again, I would have stuck to my original plan. I'm convinced that most church plants don't need a student ministry. At least in the traditional manner. I'd challenge you to have a church that reaches students, not rush out to start a separate environment.

Two years into our church, we began a weekly student ministry service. It was just time. Parents wanted it and students needed it. But those two years of learning and developing were key factors in making the decision.

DISCIPLESHIP

The first staff person that joined our staff team was a small groups pastor. Tim started working for Oak Leaf Church before we had our first service. He came without knowing what his salary would be. In fact, he raised about half of his own salary for more than a year.

Our grand opening was in August, and in October we started nine small groups. Looking back, we probably should have waited a few more months so we could develop our identity a bit more.

In Chapter ten, we'll discuss small groups and discipleship in more detail.

SERVING THE COMMUNITY

I have a conviction that Oak Leaf Church ought to make life better for everyone that lives near our church, even those who don't attend. If we packed it up and threw in the towel, there should be a bunch of people that miss us. Of course, we're not planning on going anywhere, but it would be nice to be missed if that were to happen.

When we moved to Cartersville, we decided that we were going to serve the community with no strings attached. Sure, we do a lot of things to attract attention and to try and get people to come to church. We don't apologize for that.

But we also do things just to be nice.

We want to develop a reputation of caring in this community that isn't matched by any other organization. When people think "take care of the poor," I don't want them to think of the Salvation Army, I want them to think of Oak Leaf Church. When people think about helping teachers, I don't want them to think of some foundation, I want them to think of the church.

In chapter six, I talked about some of the different community outreach projects that we've had the honor to be a part of. I think we're just scratching the surface of how we could make a difference in this county, but I want to tell you some of the ways that I believe our church has already made an impact.

One August, we asked our church to bring gift cards that we would turn around and give to teachers as school started. Somebody accused us of trying to soften up the teachers at the school we were trying to meet, but we did the same thing for another school as well. It really wasn't about advertising or brown-nosing; it was just about being nice.

In December of 2007, I really felt led to give away a week's offering. We were planning on doing it in the summer of 2008, but God really spoke to me (I use those words carefully) and told me to bump up the plan. We did not have the money, and I checked with our executive pastor every few days to make sure that we would be able to meet payroll at the end of the month.

At the conclusion of one of the services, I invited our ushers back down front and they gave envelopes to everybody in attendance. I told the church that inside the envelopes was part of an average weeks offering for us. I commissioned them to go out in the community and just serve somebody. I gave them a few ideas, but our people rose to the occasion. They went into schools and neighborhoods and just helped people.

Two weeks after we gave away that $8,300, we got an unexpected check from a church for $10,000. A couple weeks after that, a business owner in our church said that he was so moved by the experience, that his company wanted to match the gift and give it back to us. Two weeks after that, we got a hand-written note card from a lady in our church whose son had been killed in a car accident. She wanted to tithe off of the insurance money, because her son would have wanted that. We didn't give away the money for a publicity stunt, but God was faithful to us. You know, it really shouldn't surprise it when God blesses obedience.

At the conclusion of that reverse offering, we asked people to go to our website and tell their story. It's amazing to read about how God uses ordinary people to make little differences all over the place.

In early 2010, we began a monthly serving event called Second Saturday. We got the idea from another church and adapted it to fit our context. On this day, we invite everyone from our church to "show up and serve." They don't need to sign up and kids are welcome. So once a month, Oak Leafers are sent out in the community to just serve in Jesus name.

So to review, there are only five things that we try to do well at Oak Leaf Church.

Notice that developing leaders is something that stretches across all of these areas. We want to empower volunteers to lead these areas of ministry. We'll talk about that in an upcoming chapter.

I would challenge you to come up with your list. Spend time with God and determine what things He wants you to do well. Don't start something because another church does it or another blogger says it works. Don't try to do it all, focus on what God wants you to do.

CHAPTER 9:
IT FEELS LIKE IT TAKES A VILLAGE

The church is a volunteer-driven organization. At Oak Leaf Church, we rely on so many volunteers every weekend to create the environments where we can lead people from where they are to where God wants them to be.

Every now and then, in a staff meeting or from a key leader, I hear the frustration. We're knee deep in some project or task, and someone is starting to feel overwhelmed. Someone will come to me and let me know that they need more volunteers to make something happen.

I don't really have a secret list of a bunch of people with ten hours a week to spare in my desk drawer. I'm not stockpiling great people, holding on to them until a staff member who has reached the end of his rope has no way out.

I frequently remind our staff team that we have hundreds of adults who are not volunteering anywhere coming to church every week. The volunteers they need are in the building. They just have to go and get them.

If you're like most churches, you can probably rattle off three or four areas that are entering dangerous territory when it comes to volunteers. Maybe one or two of your children's classes are on shaky soil. Maybe it's gotten so bad that you're contemplating asking your wife to provide some leadership (temporarily…famous last words!). Worse yet, maybe your wife has been leading a children's class from day one even though she doesn't really want to.

Maybe you've already talked about the need to create a friendly environment and given people copies of *First Impressions,* but you find yourself in need of more greeters and ushers.

Even though you're a church of small groups and you talk about them all the time, you probably find yourself in need of more qualified small group leaders. You've already put someone in place before they were ready and they ended up leading their group through a study of the Levitical sacrificial systems before deciding that they were too deep for your church.

In this chapter, I want to give you some practical advice on getting, engaging, and keeping volunteers. We'll start with philosophy, and end up with some practical tips.

RAISE THE BAR

I am convinced that one of the major reasons our churches are not filled with volunteers is because we have set the bar too low. Our volunteer needs are not inspiring, so people sit on the sidelines.

People want to be challenged and they want to be led. They are not going to be motivated by something easy that they perceive to be unimportant. Too many times, we ask people for help with a tone of apology. We say things like:

> *Susan, I know that you're already a greeter and I know that working with kids isn't your favorite thing. But Kelly just stepped down and we really need someone to help with two-year-olds. I know it's early in the morning, and it would be hard for you to get here thirty minutes earlier, but will you think about helping us for a few months until we can find someone that really wants to do it?*

How uninspiring! That doesn't sound fun, challenging or important at all. In fact, that sounds like there's a slot that needs to be filled.

Here's how Susan should have been asked.

> *Susan, you are one of the brightest people in our church. You serve with passion and energy, and I really need your help. Every week, dozens of children are coming to learn about Jesus, and it's one of the most important areas in our church. We have an incredible opportunity to reach tons of families through our children's program. Will you pray about using your gifts of leadership in the two-year-old class? I'll email you a job description and check in on you in a few days.*

I'm not suggesting that putting on a happy face or asking big will solve all of your problems. But I am saying that we should raise the bar. We should be upfront with people when it comes to asking for their time. Don't dance around the issue if it will take five hours a week. Call for commitment. There are people in your church who want to be challenged.

It ought to mean something to be a volunteer at your church.

If Bill Hybels called me and asked me to fill in for him this weekend at Willow Creek Community Church, I wouldn't wonder how my travel was going to be reimbursed, or how much of an honorarium I would get, or how many hours it was going to take me to prepare. No way! I would feel honored to be asked, and I'd take the task to heart.

That's what musicians need to feel when they are asked to lead worship in your church. That's what adults need to feel when you entrust children to their care. Let me say it again: It ought to mean something to volunteer at your church.

CREATE A CULTURE

When we were portable, guys on our setup crew arrive at 5:00 a.m. every week and spent three hours setting up stages, speakers and two U-Haul trucks full of equipment. We did it that way from day one, and we never apologized for how early the day began.

When we ran out of power to run lights at the movie theater, they didn't tell me that we had to stop adding lights. They decided to bring a generator. I asked the setup team to get an eighteen-foot boat on the stage and the answer was "whatever you need." These guys (and ladies) went above and beyond what was necessary because that's our culture.

Creating that culture starts at the top. If you're a lazy bum, then you will not have staff and volunteers that work hard. People will only rise to the level of the leader. If you're the lead pastor, you have to lead the way for your staff.

I have to set the tone for our organization, and my staff has to keep the ball rolling. When we were portable, our entire staff arrived at 6:00 a.m. on Sunday and had setup responsibilities. I'm not going to let volunteers, who work full-time jobs during the week absorb the brunt of the work and watch the paid staff come rolling in later. Sunday morning is a workday for our staff, and our volunteers see that.

Our staff also knows that they are responsible for inviting, training, and leading their own volunteer teams. We have a connections pastor whose job is to get people connected, but it's not his job to organize every volunteer in the church. If our children's ministry needs people, then they find them and develop them. We'll share names and brainstorm together, but we hired people to lead ministry, and leading volunteers is one of the most important parts of the job.

On top of every staff member's job description is volunteer development. We constantly talk about how our job is to equip people for the work of the ministry. That's one of the most important things that we do in our job. We don't hire people to do ministry; we hire people to lead ministry.

CONNECT THE DOTS

One of our best practices is to connect the dots. People need to understand that what they do affects the bottom line mission of the church. Whenever we get a cool email or hear a great story, we're sure to pass it on to our volunteers. We let them know that they had a direct affect on someone's life.

I joke that the job of our parking team is to lead cars from where they are to where God wants them to be. I make sure that all of our Oak Leaf Kids workers know that they are teaching children about Jesus, not babysitting. I make sure our production people know that they are creating an environment for people to hear from God. They aren't watching kids, setting up projectors, or making coffee—they are helping to lead people from where they are to where God wants them to be.

You *must* connect the dots for people. They must know how their little area fits into the big picture. They must feel like their puzzle piece is important. They are not going to be motivated because of a catastrophic need. They will be motivated because of a deep vision, not because a slot needs to be filled.

Recruiting volunteers begins with vision. If you have to stand up during your services and beg for nursery workers, then you don't have a volunteer problem; you have a vision problem. In fact, we never *recruit* volunteers, we *invite* them to join us in leading people from where they are to where God wants them to be.

BE CLEAR

Andy Stanley has said this many times in many ways. You can be wrong, but you can't be unclear.

When I go to the store for my wife, I need clarity. If she tells me to get diapers, I will most certainly come home with the wrong thing. She must tell me to get *Pampers Leak Proof Dora Snuggle Pink Pull Ups, 60 pack, Size 6.*

If she didn't give me specific directions, I'd come home with Huggies. I'd technically be correct (they are diapers), but it would still be wrong.

Many of our volunteers are operating in the same way. They are doing the best they can with the tools, directions, and resources that you have given them. In an area without clear direction, they will define their roles themselves.

Volunteers want to succeed. They are not bored and trying to fill time. Deep down, they want to do something that matters. If you're not clear, then they will be left to figure it out on their own.

For this reason, we give a job description to every single volunteer within our church. This simple, one-page document lists three or four specific things that we ask them to do. Volunteers need to know who to talk to if they have problems, so we make sure their job description answers that question. If you don't tell your volunteers who their boss is, then they will come to you. Or worse, they won't go to anybody.

If an Oak Leaf Kids worker is going to be out, what do they do? Who do they call? We answer that on the job description. If a production team member needs to purchase something, who do they ask? That's on the job description.

We do not put somebody in a place of service without giving them a job description and asking if they have any questions.

All of our volunteer job descriptions are included in the Docs and Forms package, and you can get samples at *heretolead.com*.

GETTING NEW VOLUNTEERS

The best volunteers are new people to your church, who are excited about what God is doing in their lives. It's easier to train a new recruit than it is to retrain a General. If your church is on the right track, there should be new people constantly visiting your services. These people are ready to step up and want to make a difference. Your goal should be to get them connected as quickly as possible. Several times a year, we do something called Orientation. It's a quick overview of the church and we talk about ways to get connected, and the number one connection point that we emphasize is volunteering. It's routine in our church for a new person to jump into a team and start doing something right away.

SPIRITUAL GIFT TESTS

It may not be popular, but I don't really care about spiritual gift inventories or strength assessments. People generally know what they are good at if you ask them. If someone sits down with a potential volunteer and just talks to them about their family, their hobbies, their job and their favorite TV shows, my guess is that these two people could probably come up with three or four possible places of service in the church.

People don't need to take a thirty-question quiz to know that they hate working with kids. Someone that has never seen a computer doesn't need to serve on your production team. If you talk to people and ask them good questions, you'll find out where they need to go.

QUALIFY THE UNQUALIFIED

From time to time, I will make a pretty bold statement in our services. I'll say you don't even have to be a Christian to volunteer here.

While there are certain areas where this statement won't apply (Oak Leaf Kids volunteer or small group leader, for example), I don't believe people need to be Christians to help the church. We will let just about anyone join the parking team or help us setup. You don't need to be super holy to unload a trailer.

In fact, serving on these teams with other Christians who love Jesus just might be the thing that pushes someone toward following Christ.

People do not want to go through six weeks of training in order to help the church, so you better figure out some ways to let people serve quickly. I'm all for raising the bar, but there needs to be some areas where people can jump in right away. If someone called me on Friday, and said they wanted to help somewhere on Sunday, we would have three or four options for them.

TRAINING

Most people don't have dozens of hours a week to devote to learning how to be a better small group leader or greeter. Yet, it's important to provide adequate training. Here are some things that we do to provide training for volunteers.

- On-the-job training. By far, this is the most effective way to train people. If you have a new greeter, connect them with one of your great greeters and let them learn as they go. Make it the responsibility of the experienced greeter to provide training for the new greeter.
- Audio training on CD. Sit down with your staff and do a training session and put it on a CD. It's so cheap to duplicate

CDs, and you can just give them the information rather than requiring people to come to a meeting.
- Email. Your volunteers should receive communication from someone on staff a couple times a month. Once a week, I'll pick an entire team of volunteers in our church and I'll send them an encouraging email that also contains some tips. As a pastor, it's okay for you to email all the small group leaders in the church and remind them why groups are important. Email all your children's workers from time to time to thank them for all their hard work. Send an email to your production people thanking them for creating the environment where people can learn about Jesus. When you send emails, include a link to a good blog article you read that might help them grow into a better leader. Sometimes, we hoard all the good leadership information instead of sharing it. Point your leaders to good podcasts, articles, and the like.

WHAT GETS REWARDED GETS REPEATED

If you want more volunteers, then make sure you are taking care of the ones you have. Appreciate them, and you'll develop a culture that cultivates people instead of burning them out.

I really can't emphasize this enough. If you abuse people, then you'll always be short on good people. If you say thanks, and if you mean thanks, then good people will stick around.

On Monday mornings, one of the first things I do is write two or three thank you notes to volunteers that I saw doing a good job the weekend before. Sometimes I ask my staff to tell me a volunteer that is knocking it out of the park, and I'll send them a note with a Starbucks gift card. Like so many other areas, setting a thankful tone starts with the senior leader.

Once a year, we throw a big party for all of our volunteers. The first year, we put on a hoe down, complete with BBQ and a bluegrass band. We brought in a square dance caller and a dancing team and just let our people have a great time. It cost a lot of money, but it was worth it.

The next year, we threw an '80s prom. We were finishing up an '80s themed series, so it fit. We had a prom committee put it all together. There was a DJ and dancing, catered food, and decorations. We even crowned a prom king and queen. Our volunteers got all dressed up and they had a great time.

We announce these events in front of the whole church, and it just reinforces to our people that we really appreciate and value our volunteers.

We also do quarterly leadership meetings. At these one-hour events, I talk about the vision of the church. I let our leaders know where we are going before the rest of the church finds out. And at each meeting we give out a Leafy Award (our version of a Grammy) to a volunteer who has gone above and beyond and deserves special recognition.

It's a behavioral principle—what gets rewarded gets repeated. If you make a big deal out of someone or something, then chances are, somebody else will do the same thing. I'm not encouraging you to trick or bribe people, but if you are genuinely thankful, then you'll find that you have enough volunteers.

One of the simplest ways you can thank your volunteers is to send them a hand-written thank you note. I truly believe this is a lost art, but it's one of the most effective tools in your appreciation arsenal. Catch people in the act of doing something good and then write them a thank you note. I recently started writing thank you notes to kids in our church. Last year, a married couple in our church taught about finances. Instead of sending them a thank you note, I sent it to their kids. It said, "Hey, I know you already know this but you have really awesome parents. They stood up in front of every adult in our church and talked about being faithful with money. You are really blessed to have parents like that. Here's a Coldstone gift card…take your really cool parents out for ice cream."

I routinely get thank you notes back for thank you notes. I don't exactly know how that cycle should end. Should I send another thank you note saying thanks for their thank you note? It just goes to show you that people are under-appreciated, and that as leaders, we have an incredible opportunity to appreciate people.

LEADERS ARE PASTORS

When a person is on a volunteer team, I know that they have a relationship with a leader in our church who will care for them. In a way, every one of our volunteer leaders are like pastors. They pastor a small group of volunteers. Obviously, these teams are task-oriented. They greet before the 10:00 a.m. service, they work in the parking lot, and they play in the band. But the leader of each team knows that they are spiritually responsible for them on some level. What if you make your volunteer teams kind of like a small group? Add prayer and community to the mix. Get together once a month for dinner and talk about life. Teams of volunteers *can* function like small groups in that sense, and community *can* develop.

CHAPTER 10:
GROUPS AND CLASSES

Two months after starting our church, we started small groups. We were quickly able to connect a large percentage of our adult attenders into groups. But over the next few years, that percentage fell off. We sat in meetings wondering what we could do to get more people connected to a small group. Three years into it, I realized that we were asking the wrong question. We were trying to figure out how to get people into a group, when we should have been asking about how to get people to take a step in discipleship. Groups were the strategy, but not the goal.

In our evaluation, we came to believe that groups were not going to be the discipleship mechanism for 100 percent of our people. For various reasons, lots of people in our church would not or could not join a group. Furthermore, we began to realize that groups may not be cut out for everyone. Please hear what I am saying. I am *not* saying that community, Bible study, and accountability are not for everyone; the church *must* pursue those things. But groups as the vehicle might not work well for everyone.

For many people, especially people who are relationally driven, groups work well. But for others, perhaps those who are more thoughtful or introverted, classes might be better.

So, in the summer of 2009, we ran a test program called Oak Leaf University. This was a series of six-week classes that met for two hours on Tuesday nights. Instead of group discussion, we had experienced teachers deliver content in more of a classroom setting. We taught theology in one class and Introduction to the New Testament in another. People loved these classes and we expanded the program.

Some people are built to learn in a classroom setting, while others need a more relational framework for Bible study. We believe that through Journey Groups and Oak Leaf University, we can provide a next step in discipleship for the majority of our people. We realized that we would need both of these formats.

So, let's discuss these two discipleship environments. First up: groups. Here's why groups are so important at Oak Leaf Church:

1. We believe life change happens best in smaller groups. Our weekend services are designed to help people take steps in their faith, but groups are the place where people can make huge strides.

2. Groups are the most relevant thing we can do. Modern churches like ours often use music, lights and media to present the gospel in a relevant way. But when you think about it, groups are the most relevant thing we offer. When a person is going through a struggle or has questions about faith, what can be more relevant than a group of people coming alongside them and helping them out?

3. People get cared for in groups. In a large church, it's impossible to know the needs of everyone. As the lead pastor, I rarely hear about who is sick or who is looking for a job. And if all those needs did make it all the way to me, I might become paralyzed with the sheer enormity of them all. But when someone is in a group, they have a family that can care for them, help meet their needs, show up to help them move, visit their newborn in the hospital, take them food in a time of need, and much more.

4. Groups are just as much church as what we do on the weekend. When people get together to pray and study the Bible, that's just as much church as when they get together to sing and hear a sermon on the weekend.

5. Groups make a big church smaller. Sometimes, people leave our church because they didn't make a connection. Sometimes, people get mad because they don't have my cell phone number or nobody on staff knew about their issues. While I wish that wasn't the case, it's impossible for me to know everyone in our church. Even after two years, we have more than thirty-five hundred people in our database and nearly one thousand people attending every weekend. The bottom line is that we may not know you're there on a weekend, and we may not notice when you're missed. But if you're in a group of some sort, you will be known and you will be missed. When you're in a group, you've got a relationship and a responsibility.

By the way, some of the coldest, most impersonal churches are the fifty person churches where everybody knows everybody and you're there as an outsider. It has nothing to do with size, but everything to do with who you know.

6. It seems to be the model of the early church. Jesus had the 12 disciples, and spent a lot of time with those guys. The book of Acts describes the early church meeting in homes, eating together, learning together and growing in their faith together. We think groups are a great way to go from where you are to where God wants you to be.

7. Groups are efficient and effective. As a young church, we didn't have a typical church building. This made something like Sunday school (which wasn't invented until the 1700s) pretty tough. Sunday school can be a great way to grow in your faith, but so can groups. We don't have to build gigantic educational buildings and have capital campaigns to teach people how to follow Jesus. People can simply open their homes and open their Bibles. It's very cost effective, and the meeting places are really limitless!

8. Groups are great for developing leaders. Jesus said that if we're faithful in the small areas, he will trust us with more. Groups is a great way for leaders in Oak Leaf Church to care for people, pray for people, and teach people how to follow Jesus. In a way, group leaders are like pastors. All of our group leaders have coaches, and our connections pastor works hard to help people become better leaders.

As a young church, we have about 35 to 40 percent of our adults involved in a small group. We don't consider the three ladies that come into the office to fold the weekly handout a small group just to get a better percentage. For us, a small group meets on a regular basis to go through a Bible study. Four guys meeting on Mondays to play poker doesn't count.

I think these are a few key components to small groups in a church plant, though this is certainly not an exhaustive list.

TEACH ABOUT THEM

We mention small groups constantly from our stage. I'll allude to them in messages and we'll tell cool stories that we hear. But a couple of times a year, I will teach an entire message on small groups. This usually happens before a kickoff event. These messages are great opportunities to talk about Biblical community.

GETTING INTO GROUPS

At first, we borrowed the *GroupLink* concept from North Point Community Church, hosting a two-hour event designed to connect people in a group right there on the spot. It worked well for us at first, but as our church changed, we realized that starting groups once a year didn't really match our open culture. Now, we emphasize groups two times a year, but we make the group lists public on our website. People can join a group anytime, and group leaders are always looking for people to connect with their group. In January and in August, I'll really emphasize groups from the stage, and this point of emphasis will lead lots of new people into lots of new groups.

LEADERSHIP DEVELOPMENT

I think the key to effective small groups is leadership development. A group that has a weak leader will not make it. In fact, they will hurt your church.

If you're like most people, you'll have a hard time getting everyone together for training sessions. Leadership retreats are tough to schedule and people are busy. But it's pretty easy to send regular training emails to group leaders. The person who oversees our small groups communicates to group leaders via email, and as the lead pastor, I do the same thing.

I also record a leadership podcast and we send that to our leaders. These ten to fifteen minute sessions provide some quick training for our leaders. Since all of them don't do podcasts, we put them on a CD as well.

It's important that our group leaders understand the vision of the church. For that reason, we don't put people in leadership lightly. We want them to be in a healthy group for at least six months before they lead one, even if they have come from another church. I'd actually say *especially* if they have come from another church.

I'd rather have a group that is too large, than to divide and let a premature leader take a group. Nobody is perfect, but it's necessary that a group leader be a growing Christian who supports the leadership of the church.

Hands down, there is one thing that group leaders must understand. Out of all the qualifications for being a group leader, understanding the vision of the church is the most important. If you have a group leader that is slightly misaligned, that will hurt the effectiveness of your whole group strategy. Group leaders need to be sold out to the vision of the church. They cannot bring in their personal philosophies on what groups should be like. This is why group leaders from other churches might not make the best group leaders at your church.

Make sure your group leaders understand and buy into the vision for the church and your strategy for groups.

VOLUNTEER TEAMS CAN WORK LIKE GROUPS

Though a volunteer team is not the same as a small group, there are ways to make volunteer teams function like groups. In other words, a volunteer team can build community. Here's some ways that we encourage volunteer teams to connect people:

- Make sure volunteers on the team have each other's contact information.
- Send a weekly email with information, but also include prayer requests.
- Get together a few times a year for something fun.
- Visit another church service together.
- Go to a conference together.

- Serve in the community together. Preschool workers could help with a school's fall festival. The band could help with a community concert.
- Go on a mission trip together.

When someone in our church is connected to a volunteer team, we know that they are going to be cared for, prayed for ,and developed by a lead volunteer. That's a win for us!

CLASSES

At the beginning of the chapter, I mentioned a program we started in 2009 called Oak Leaf University. Each "semester," we offer five or six classes. After our test semester we decided that six weeks was a little long, so a class lasts four weeks, and it meets for two hours on a weeknight. There's a thirty-minute break in the middle, and with all the classes breaking at the same time, this creates opportunity for conversations to happen naturally. Since the classes are four weeks, we can run several semesters a year, and still take a week or two off in between. This gives us multiple launching points and new people always have something new to attend.

Oak Leaf University has eight core classes, and we're writing the curriculum for each course. Here's the core track:

- Theology – Theology is the study of God, and in this course, we cover several major doctrines of the faith.
- Parenting – in this class, we talk about how to lead your child to Jesus, how to talk to them about sex and how to discipline them effectively.
- Introduction to the Old Testament – this is a survey course of the Old Testament. It's like a seminary class for the every day person.
- Introduction to the New Testament – we walk through the message of the New Testament in this class.
- Spiritual Disciplines – this class focuses on prayer, Bible reading, Scripture memory and some other spiritual disciplines.
- Biblical Finances – we cover topics like debt, savings, giving, insurance, and budgeting.

- Intentional Living (Evangelism) – this class answers the question, "How do I share my faith?"
- Leadership – this is a basic leadership class, and it's appropriate for leaders in our church, but is also applicable for business, school, and life. This class gives us a great way to take our key leaders to the next level.

There's a teacher guide and a student guide for each class, which are much like college classes driven by information. You might wonder, "How do you keep the classes interesting and fun?" Well, that all depends on the teacher. Great teachers know how to present important information in an engaging way. Though the class isn't discussion-based, great teachers know how to get the class to interact with each other and with the material.

SUMMARY

Our discipleship strategy involves *teams, groups, and classes*. We believe all three of these are required because one size does not fit all. Introverts who may not connect with a group have the opportunity to grow in their faith by taking a class. Busy people can still find Biblical community by being a part of a volunteer team. In Orientation, we present all three of these and let people know that the next step is up to them. Here's how it looks:

120 *From The Top Down*

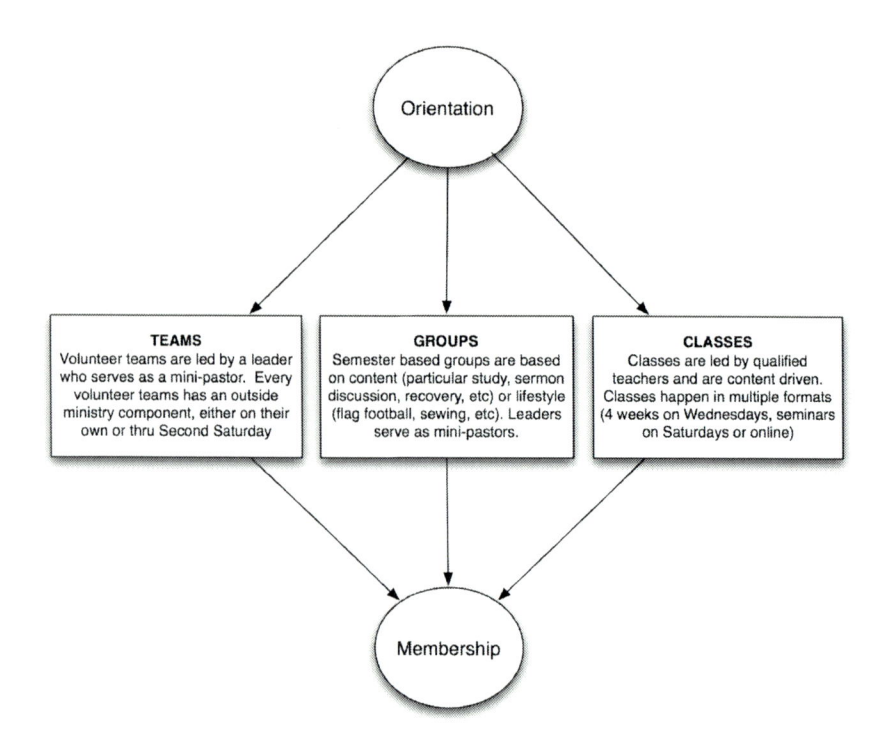

```
                    ┌─────────────┐
                    │ Orientation │
                    └──────┬──────┘
          ┌────────────────┼────────────────┐
          ▼                ▼                ▼
```

TEAMS	**GROUPS**	**CLASSES**
Volunteer teams are led by a leader who serves as a mini-pastor. Every volunteer teams has an outside ministry component, either on their own or thru Second Saturday	Semester based groups are based on content (particular study, sermon discussion, recovery, etc) or lifestyle (flag football, sewing, etc). Leaders serve as mini-pastors.	Classes are led by qualified teachers and are content driven. Classes happen in multiple formats (4 weeks on Wednesdays, seminars on Saturdays or online)

```
          └────────────────┼────────────────┘
                           ▼
                    ┌─────────────┐
                    │ Membership  │
                    └─────────────┘
```

CHAPTER 11:
ON BEING PORTABLE

At the time when this chapter was written Oak Leaf Church was meeting at a movie theater. We met at a movie theater, then moved to a high school, and then moved back to the movie theater. We now meet at a renovated nightclub that we purchased in 2008.

Oak Leaf Church is a portable church. I love being a portable church, and the thought of shelling out millions of dollars right now to build a building is not very exciting to me.

Portability is a part of our vision. When we first started, I told people that doing church in the middle of the marketplace will always be a part of our DNA. We don't want to build a giant structure and make people come to us; we want to take church to where the people are.

Before our church even held its first service, thousands of people were in our building. People knew where our church was located because most of them had been to see a movie. Guests knew where the sanctuary was because they saw Gollum there.

Being portable is all about the vision. There are a ton of portable churches that struggle because the leadership doesn't communicate the *why* behind the *what*. Your staff and volunteers need to know that portability is a part of your DNA; it's not a stepping-stone toward becoming a real church.

If you visit most church websites and find the history tab, you'll find a history of buildings. The history is tied to the construction of the first building, to the expansion of the sanctuary, to the addition of the Family Life Center.

Our church thrives on being portable, and it has never been an excuse for why we couldn't do something. Being portable has never kept us from doing something that God has wanted us to do. In fact, it forces us to be creative when it comes to planning events and services.

Our church buys into portability because I buy into it. I do not spend all of my time dreaming about facilities or talking about how great it would be if we had a building. In fact, I do just the opposite. I take every opportunity I can to talk about being salt and light in the world. I remind people that the very service they are attending is an example of that principle. As a leader, love the fact that you're portable. Don't rush your church into a building project or massive debt just so you don't have to setup speakers on Sunday morning.

I'm proud of the vibe that our team creates in the movie theater on Sunday morning. It has the look and feel of a movie theater, but it has our personality too. I think we do portable church in a theater as well as anyone. I can say that with integrity, because it has nothing to do with me—it's all because of our team.

CHOOSING A PORTABLE LOCATION

There are church plants meeting in all kinds of facilities: movie theaters, high school auditoriums, elementary school cafeterias, bars, nightclubs, restaurants, YMCAs, other churches, coffee shops, houses and more. Any place with space is a potential home for a church plant.

Movie theaters and schools are two common places for churches to meet. In our first eighteen months, we've utilized both of these facilities as meeting places, and there are pros and cons to both.

superintendent and the school board lawyer to hammer out the details. The assistant superintendent looked at our executive pastor and said, "You guys have proved me wrong."

I consider that one of our biggest wins as a church. We made a few mistakes at the school (messed with a few lights that we shouldn't have moved and had food in one room where it was not allowed). Each time we made mistakes, we owned up to them and fixed them. Never promise someone that there won't be problems, but promise that when problems arise, you'll go over the top to make things right.

In 2009, after we had moved back to the movie theater, we had reached our seating capacity at the movie theater. We already had three services on Sunday morning, but we felt like if we provided more seats for people, then God would send them.

So we started a fourth service, setting up two identical theaters for adults and overlapping the start times. Four separate services across two theaters in a movie theater on Sunday morning. We setup two stages, two sound systems, and two lighting rigs. We had two bands, and I moved from theater to theater teaching. It was a crazy schedule! We could not have attempted something like this without having a great relationship with local management.

PORTABLE CHILDREN'S ENVIRONMENTS

Setting up for children at the movie theater was tough in the early days. We didn't have much money, so our classrooms were a collection of portable walls borrowed from another church, a bunch of blue Rubbermaid bins, and toys and supplies purchased from garage sales and consignment shops. I wished we had the money to bring in Portable Church Industries and do things right, but we just didn't. We setup in the hallways of the movie theater because we couldn't afford to rent additional theaters.

Over the course of the first few months, when we could afford to rent additional theaters, we went to upgrade our children's facilities. Because the theaters were pretty dark (and many of the house lights were burned out), we brought in shop lights and set them up in the back of the theater. We traded out the plain rugs we got from the discount carpet outlet for some soft, foam flooring. We ditched the Rubbermaid bins for some quality cases from Portable Church Industries (we only had money to buy some used ones). We setup pipe and drape in the kids theaters and printed colorful banners to hang.

Elementary children loved coming to church at the theater. We used KidMo, which is a DVD-based material. We setup a projector and just projected onto the giant movie screen. After the teaching and singing times, kids would break into small groups. It was a very basic setup, but our leaders made it fun. Since the elementary environment is called the City, our leaders brought in a bunch of road signs and lined the hallway. They brought in additional lights and a small stage. We used banners and backdrops to help create an identity.

In both the preschool and elementary environments, we started with what we had and improved something every week. Even though we didn't spend much money, we still made it look good.

To check-in children, we used a simple label system. After about a year, we moved to a computerized check-in system, which made things look professional. Looking back, I wish we had moved to the computerized check-in earlier. It's worth the investment and communicates quality and excellence to parents, even before they enter the classrooms.

Most of our children's workers had setup responsibilities. Since we were a portable church, we didn't have kids workers that showed up five minutes before the service. Most of these committed volunteers arrived early to setup the environments. The crew that worked in the last service stayed to tear it down and pack it up. I really believe that the best volunteers in your church should be working in your kid's areas.

MUST HAVE STUFF

There's some great stuff that won't work because it's not portable. We made mistakes building things that turned out to be too heavy, so we couldn't use it. We bought stuff that didn't hold up over a couple of weeks. When you get stuff, you have to ask yourself how it's going to work in a portable application.

SETTING THE BAR HIGH

Every church has to cut corners. I would challenge you *not* to cut the corners that the majority of people see on Sunday morning.

We pay our staff once a month instead of twice a month, because that saves us $720 in payroll expenses. I ask them to do that so we can spend the money on the weekend or on community outreach.

We don't print a bunch of stuff in the office in order to save paper; we read it off computer screens. But when we print stuff for our people, it's in full color and it looks good.

When things get tight financially, we ask our staff to eliminate all meal expenses (taking people out to eat). That's cutting a corner that only affects one or two people.

It takes a lot of money to run a portable church well, but it's not nearly the cost of owning your own building. Spend the money on nice cases and totes; your volunteers will thank you. Spend the money on nice video cameras; go without something for a while and save up if you have to. Doing things with excellence costs more money, but prioritize your list and start knocking things off.

EVALUATE RUTHLESSLY

If you want to create excellent environments and have excellent services, you're going to have to commit to a ruthless evaluation. You need to walk through your lobby and look at things through the eyes of a guest. You need to bring in consultants from the outside that will pick up on things that you miss. Watch your services on video and see what could look better. Ask your volunteers what they think needs attention. Ask guests what they thought.

Excellence does not happen by accident. You must be intentional and ruthless. If your environment has looked the same for a while, maybe it's time to look at things with fresh eyes. What can you do better? What signs do you need to update? What needs improvement?

CHAPTER 12:
GETTING THE RIGHT PEOPLE ON THE BUS

I moved to Cartersville, Georgia somewhat reluctantly. Cartersville really isn't well known, and it's not the hub of anything. Unless you count meth labs.

This town wasn't really receptive to the idea of a new church. The other churches in this town weren't really receptive of another church either. I got an email from one pastor who literally told me that this city didn't really need a new church…someone had tried that a few years back and it didn't really work.

I got a lot of funny looks from business owners and community leaders. People could understand building church buildings and the construction industry, but the idea of starting a church with no people, no money, and no building was out of control. Even though I assured them that the need was legitimate, when I told people that I was a church planter, they looked at me like I had just said my name was George Costanza and I worked for Vandelay Industries.

We didn't know anyone in this town so getting people to join the launch team was tough. Getting people to join the staff was even tougher. This anti-church town that was filled with churches was the backdrop for where I would find my first staff person.

MAKING THE FIRST HIRE

Most of the books I read and conferences I attended spoke about the importance of hiring a worship pastor as soon as possible. Nearly every sample budget I saw included money for a lead pastor and worship pastor. Since that's what smart people said I should do, that's what I set out to do.

I called every friend I knew. I visited several mid-week college worship services. I scouted at local colleges. I tried to persuade worship leader friends to move to Cartersville and help me start a church.

But I kept coming up empty. I discovered that musicians are a dime a dozen (everybody can play "Freebird" on the guitar), but a qualified, gifted, and called worship leader is hard to find. Time kept ticking, and I kept searching.

At one point, I thought I would have to be the lead pastor and the Worship Leader so I dusted off my guitar and starting reliving my days as a youth pastor/worship leader. I didn't think that this church should be singing "Trading My Sorrows" or "Stairway to Heaven" every week, so I got over this phase pretty quickly.

As it got closer to launch day, I just gave up on the worship leader search and focused my energies elsewhere. If we didn't have a worship leader, then I'd just hire an entire band and pretend like they are our band.

It was during this time that I realized that we should be playing to our strengths. For whatever reason, God wasn't bringing us this worship leader, but he was working in another area.

When I first moved to town, I called a few youth pastors to track down the names of some good teenage babysitters. One of these youth pastors was Tim. We ended up meeting one morning at Cracker Barrel and talking shop. It turns out that Tim was slightly frustrated at the direction his church was headed, and he began praying about joining our team.

I didn't want this to happen at all. I didn't want to be known for stealing church members, much less, stealing staff. Tim felt God leading him to step down from his church and put his house up for sale. All this without any promise of a job from Oak Leaf Church.

In the end, Tim became our first staff member. He started taking care of all kinds of things for us – organizing outreach events, calling guests, meeting with potential volunteers. A few months into it, we decided that Tim should have a title so we called him our connections pastor.

Two months after we launched, we began small groups, and about 100 people connected to a group.

Since we didn't have a worship pastor on staff, we played to our strengths. We had good music on Sundays because we were bringing in bands, but our staff was able to focus on getting people to show up for church and helping them connect once they did.

I know people say that the worship pastor might be the first position you fill, but I think it's more important to hire people, not positions. Play to your strengths.

HIRING FROM WITHIN

Tim started serving at Oak Leaf Church before he had a paycheck, and that's been the pattern for nearly every person that we have hired. Our preference is to hire people from within our church. This has several advantages:

- We are able to see their heart.
- We are able to see their work ethic.
- They are able to see our vision at work.
- The interview and transition process is much simpler.

When we hire from within, we look for people currently serving in our church. If they are serving Jesus out of a love for Him and a passion for the church, then that's a good sign. We run from someone who will not get involved unless there is a paycheck.

When we hire from within, we are affirming that a love for Jesus and a commitment to this church is more important than education. Very few of the people on our staff have college or seminary degrees in their particular field. Before starting this church, I had no idea what it meant to be a pastor. Our executive pastor was a schoolteacher. Our small groups pastor was a youth pastor. Our creative arts pastor knew how to lead worship (which is a plus for a worship leader), but he'd never been a creative arts pastor at a church before.

When we hire from within, we are saying that a commitment to leadership development is more important than experience. We hire leaders, and leaders can do a variety of things in our church, because the principles are not the same. Someone can learn how to run a children's ministry by attending some conferences, reading some books, and setting up some meetings. But it's tough to learn how to develop and inspire people. We look for that second trait because we know we can develop the first one.

Nearly everybody that has joined our staff has come from within our church. They were attenders, members and volunteers serving in ministry before they were officially on staff. The first person we brought in from the outside only lasted a few months because he didn't fit our culture.

THE HIRING PROCESS

During our first couple of years as a church, we have really refined our hiring process. While we were a little free flowing at first, now we really do homework on potential hires. I think it ought to be as hard to get a job at Oak Leaf Church as it is to run for Congress. Here's a list of the steps we take when hiring someone:

1. Create job profile. This is not a job description, but a profile of the position. We tweak job descriptions based on the strengths of the employee, but the profile describes what we're looking for in a person.
2. Receive resumes. Occasionally, we'll post a job on some of the job boards, and when we do that, we're flooded with resumes.
3. Complete a preliminary questionnaire. We send ten questions to people that look normal and ask them to answer them via email.
4. Phone conversation. Someone from our Lead Team will have a phone conversation with the person.
5. Job Application. Our job application is pretty thorough and includes permission to run a background check and a credit report. And yes, we do those things.
6. Follow-up phone call conversation. I'll participate in this conversation.

7. Check references, especially their previous employer. We will never hire someone without checking his or her references. If we can't find out about a weakness, then we'll keep digging.
8. Ask previous church about giving. I want to know that this person gave to their last church. We expect all of our staff to give, and if they weren't doing it at their last church, we put on the breaks. If the person is coming from within, we look at their giving records. If they aren't giving as a volunteer, they won't give as a staff member.
9. Discuss salary and benefits.
10. Background and credit check. At this point, we will pull these reports and talk about anything we find.
11. In-person interviews with Lead Team. We get other people from our team involved in the interview process because we believe that everybody is smarter than somebody.
12. Sit down with Lead Team and spouses. My wife is a great judge of personality and fit, so as we're getting close to the end of the process, we get the wives involved. We don't hire someone to get free work from his or her spouse, but ministry is a team effort.
13. Professional counselors evaluation. This is an over the top step, but if the person is coming to us from outside our area, we pay for a professional counselor to talk with them.
14. Offer job.

As you can see, our process is pretty thorough. It didn't used to be that way, but we have a very high regard for what it means to be on staff at Oak Leaf Church. After the person is officially hired, here are the steps we go through to ensure a good transition.

1. Review employee handbook and sign paperwork. This includes a confidentiality agreement.
2. Payroll information. We do direct deposits so we get all that setup.
3. Create the staff email address.
4. Fellowship One login and training.
5. One-month evaluation with supervisor.
6. Six-month evaluation with supervisor where job description is reviewed and revised.

STAFF DEVELOPMENT

We look for leaders, because we know that people with the gift of leadership can lead people and learn the necessary skills. I can teach someone how to organize small groups, but I cannot teach someone how to build into people.

Once you find people crazy enough to join the staff of a church plant, it's time to go to work developing them.

- During our weekly all-staff meeting, there is always a time of leadership development. Sometimes, we all read the same book and talk about the principles we learned. Other times, we ask staff members to read a leadership book or something pertaining to their area and bring four or five takeaways. Throughout the year, I ask other pastors and leaders to come talk to our staff about leadership.
- I send out an all-staff email every Monday morning. It contains some statistics from the previous weekend and some upcoming event information, but I usually build in some kind of leadership lesson.
- We talk about leadership lessons in our weekly Lead Team meeting.
- We go to a couple of conferences as a staff, and we make sure that every staff member has money in the budget to go to a ministry specific conference.
- Once a year we do Staff Advance, a three-day all-staff retreat. We make goals for the next year, and discuss other big picture items. And we just have fun hanging out and spending time together outside of the office.

PAYING STAFF

In October, our Lead Team goes to work on building the budget for the next year. And about half of that budget is allocated to personnel. Staff is a giant part of what we hope to accomplish at Oak Leaf Church. We'd rather spend money on people than programs, because good people will make a lasting impact.

The first thing we did when getting serious about this was join The National Association of Church Business Administrators (NACBA). This organization produces a detailed report of salary information. You can see what lead pastors, worship pastors, youth pastors, administrative assistants, and people in other church positions in churches your size make. You can sort the data by church size, budget, denomination, or state. This information is very helpful to us. It lets us know what churches in our financial position pay their staff.

The NACBA staffing report breaks salaries down into percentages. Our goal as a church is to pay people in the seventy-fifth percentile of their bracket. In other words, we want to pay people well.

Right now, our entire staff makes somewhere in the twenty-fifth percentile range. We're systematically trying to move people up the ladder.

After consulting this report, we go to work making tweaks and changes. We take stage of life and overall value to our church into consideration. It may not be normal, but we don't pay people more because they have been to seminary or have a college degree.

How do we set specific salaries? The Board of Directors sets my salary. I always want to make sure I am above reproach when it comes to handling the money. Money gets a lot of church leaders into trouble and I just don't want to go there.

During the budgeting process, our executive pastor gathers the information from NACBA and pairs that with all the financial data from our church (offerings, projected budget, etc.) and sends that to the others pastors and church leaders on our Board of Directors. They come back with a specific number. Our executive pastor takes those numbers and works with them for a few weeks, and then the Board of Directors signs off on the final number. That's my salary for the upcoming calendar year, and I stay out of it.

I set the salaries of all other staff members, in consultation with our executive pastor. We look at the NACBA reports for each position and look at the monthly job evaluations and six-month evaluations to come up with their salaries.

In addition to salaries, those on our Lead Team also receive some benefits. We give everyone a certain dollar amount to use for benefits. They could use the amount on insurance or retirement and allocate it however they like.

IT'S NOT FAIR

If you've got kids, you've probably heard the phrase "that's not fair." Kids are fascinated with fairness when they think they are being shortchanged. Adults are often the same way.

One summer, we went to obtain a special permit to hand out bottled water at an intersection. We wanted to get an intersection where the Shriners always collect money, but we were told that intersection wasn't open. According to the police department, they must have had a variance. We asked the city about obtaining a variance and were told that one wasn't possible. The Shriners weren't supposed to collect money there, and we couldn't hand out water there.

We finally got permission to hand out the water at a less-crowded intersection, and we ended up giving away more than one thousand bottles of water. A couple of weeks later, I saw the Shriners collecting money at the intersection I originally wanted and I was ticked. We were denied, so it was only fair that they be kicked out. I actually called the police. When the police station asked my name, I gave the lady the name of our small groups pastor. I'm all for the Shriners, but something in me just screamed out "that's not fair." I'm probably just bitter.

The bottom line is that when it comes to salaries at Oak Leaf Church, we're not fair. We don't pay everyone the same amount of money, and there are a lot of factors that go into setting someone's salary. A new employee may be paid more than an old employee because of the job requirements or the level of responsibility. When setting salaries, I consider replacement value: What would it cost me to replace this person? Not the position, but the person.

We have a rule on our staff: we don't talk about our salaries. In fact, it's something that will get you fired. Everybody that works with us signs a confidentiality agreement, and we take that very seriously.

We use the NACBA reports and our own internal values in setting individual salaries. It's not fair, but some positions on staff are more important than other positions. They bring more to the table, and they actually make other staff positions possible. Just like you may go through a process of ranking your core values, you might want to go through a process of prioritizing your ministries.

VALUE STAFF

One of the reasons that our hiring process is so tough is because we really value our staff. Being on staff at Oak Leaf Church is a big deal to me, and the people on the team should be treated like family.

As a church plant, we couldn't really lure people in with big salaries, but we worked hard to create a dynamic culture. I've already talked about our goal of getting people to the seventy-fifth percentile in regards to average salary for their position. But there are many other things you can do to value your staff. Here are a few ideas.

1. **Use credit card rewards points to give staff bonuses.** We pay for everything we can with a Visa card and we use the reward dollars to give out some staff bonuses. One year on the week after Easter, we took everyone on staff down to the mall and gave them a $75 gift card and told them to get something for themselves. Afterwards, we ate lunch and went bowling. It was a fun way to blow off steam, and it was worth the money.
2. **Give out a gift card as a prize for a good report.** In our all-staff meeting, we go around the room giving reports. Sometimes, I'll give out a gift card for the best report.
3. **Ask people's opinions.** You'll be amazed at how far asking for a simple opinion before taking action will go in building team morale. People want to know that their opinions are valued. The person over your production might have a great insight about children's ministry.
4. **Include spouses when you can.** We pay for spouses to attend the staff/spouse retreat each summer. We look for ways to intentionally involve spouses.

LETTING PEOPLE GO

Chances are, you're going to let someone go. Maybe it will be a character issue or a competence issue. Sometimes, great people just don't fit and you decide to go in a different direction. In our short history, this has happened to us.

Life is too short and the mission of the church is too important to struggle through fit issues. If someone isn't a good fit for your staff, you could also be holding them back from fulfilling their mission. It's a two-way street.

Here are a few helpful hints for when you decide to part ways:

1. Honesty is the best policy. Don't string people along. Be clear and forthcoming with your expectations.
2. Take care of people financially. If you're letting someone go, give him or her a generous severance so they can transition to their next place. It's better to err on the side of "too much" than "too little."
3. Both employer and employee should sign a resignation or termination agreement. This puts all the expectations down on paper and produces clarity. The agreement should include what information will be public and what will remain private.
4. Protect the staff person, and ask the staff person to protect the church. For us, protecting the church has to happen or the severance package won't take effect. The church is more important than anyone's feelings.

CHAPTER 13:
PARTING SHOT

Jesus said that He would build the church. While I tell people that Oak Leaf Church was officially born on August 20, 2006, it was really born in eternity past in the mind of God. I can't even really grasp that.

The church is God's plan for spreading the Gospel. Jesus entrusted his message to the disciples who went throughout the known world telling His story. As they did, churches were formed. For thousands of years, the church has advanced. There are those who would say that the church is doomed, but we know otherwise. Throughout dark times, the church has endured. She will continue to endure because she belongs to the eternal God. No matter how many studies George Barna releases, the church will endure.

The church is the vehicle that Jesus will use to carry his message to the ends of the world. For this reason, I believe church planting to be one of the most effective ways to spread the gospel. Starting new churches—effective churches—is one of the best ways to advance the Kingdom. We need more churches. We need churches in cities and churches out in the country. We need more ethnic churches. We need more churches with rock bands and we need churches with choirs. We need traditional churches and contemporary. Whenever people figure what emergent churches really are, we could use more of those too.

I have a special place in my heart for church planters. If you're praying about planting a church, if you're crazy enough to quit your job and set out on an adventure, if you're willing to call yourself a pastor even though you have no people or building, you're a member of a special fraternity. You're on the front lines of ministry.

Church planters are crazy. You're out of your mind for even considering it. But God uses crazy. God uses bold. God appreciates audacity and answers audacious prayers.

The ocean of church planting might be rough, but when you decide to launch a sailboat, you'll find that there's no other place you'd rather be.

APPENDIX 1:
52 OFFERING TALK IDEAS

1. Teaching: If God wants your money, he'll take it.
2. Teaching: I don't need your money, but you need to give it.
3. Vision: Video highlights or pictures from Second Saturday.
4. Teaching: You haven't really worshipped until you've given.
5. Information: Video from Verve (church plant we support).
6. Teaching: It's not really giving unless you miss it.
7. Teaching: We are not owners, we're managers.
8. Vision: What God is doing upstairs in kid's ministry.
9. Teaching: Giving is trusting.
10. Teaching: Where we allocate money is a representation of what is really important to us.
11. Teaching: You've been blessed because somebody else gave.
12. Vision: Video of what kids are learning in their classes, followed by "that's why we give."
13. Teaching: The woman with the alabaster jar worshipped through giving.
14. Teaching: "I will not offer sacrifices to God that cost me nothing."
15. Teaching: Giving is a form of worship.
16. Information: Where the money goes chart. 46% staff. 24% ministry, etc.

17. Vision: Do giving talk right after baptism. "We give so we can see life change."
18. Vision: Video of kids saying why they love their church.
19. Vision: A volunteer testimony: "Here's why I give to this church."
20. Vision: Video of student ministry "We invest in the next generation."
21. Teaching: You have to plan to be generous—Is. 32:8.
22. Teaching: Be thankful—Ps 50:13, Luke 17:15-16.
23. Information: Our community partners. When you give to Oak Leaf Church, you're also helping organizations around our city.
24. Information: Video from Axiom Church (church plant we support).
25. Information: Video from The Gallery Church (church plant we support).
26. Information: Video from Emmaus (church plant we support).
27. Vision: Read an email we received thanking our church.
28. Teaching: Playing monopoly—when it's over, it all goes back in the box. Don't just buy houses and hotels; invest in the Kingdom.
29. Teaching: What is marginally important (stuff here) vs. what is eternally important.
30. Vision: What God is doing through small groups.
31. Vision: Video highlights or pictures from The Egg Drop.
32. Information: Three ways to give: in the service, online, at a kiosk.
33. Video: Another pastor thanking Oak Leaf Church for investing in other church plants.
34. Video: Staff around the office (freezing or burning up) illustrates that the staff is concerned with leveraging their resources to do more ministry.
35. Vision: Testimonials from financial counseling.
36. Video/Teaching: store treasure in heaven—film video at a new car lot and end up in the rusted junkyard (Matthew 6:19).
37. Information: Graphs illustrating YTD budget needs/surplus—discuss future needs.
38. Information: Video/Slideshow connecting our total income with all the other life change numbers for the year

39. Information: Money saving tips video.
40. Teaching: Where your money there your heart will be also. What's the first thing you do when you get paid? Are you thinking how can I spend or how can I give?
41. Teaching: Blessings of God follow obedience.
42. Vision: Video of someone talking about how their small group has helped them grow in their faith.
43. Vision: Video that tracks $1 from an offering bucket – counting-bank-website-box arrives – invites purchased placed on wall-invite taken-invite handed out-new person shows up at church with invite in hand.
44. Vision: Give the offering back to people and ask them to go bless their neighbors.
45. Information: Video from staff thanking people for their support
46. Vision: Explain a chart showing how many unchurched people there are in our area.
47. Vision: Video of a volunteer saying why they give their time.
48. Vision: Map of U.S.A./World with dots showing church plants and missions we are supporting. Talk about how local giving becomes global giving.
49. Vision: Tell people what you already did with the offering. "Because you guys give faithfully, last month we were able to send money to build a well in Africa. We're not taking up a special offering today, because you already gave. Great job!"
50. Information: Globalrichlist.com. You are already rich.
51. Teaching/Vision: 1 Tim 6:17-18. If 100 people represented the world: 53 would live on $2 a day. If you have a monthly income of at least $4,000, then you are making 100 times more than the average person on this planet. Which is more messed up: That we have so much compared to everyone else or that we don't think we are rich?
52. Vision: Read a list of names of people who have prayed to receive Christ. What do these names have in common? They all made decisions to follow Christ this last month.

APPENDIX 2:
WHAT'S INCLUDED ON THE DOCS AND FORMS CD

ADMINISTRATION DOCUMENTS

Monthly Snapshot
Statement of Beliefs
Bylaws
Job description for Board of Directors
Head Count Sheet
Ordination Application
Calendar Request Form
Descriptions of Meetings and Retreats
Staff Organization Chart
Event Planning Checklist
Travel Guide
Processes

FACILITIES DOCUMENTS

Facility Use Policy
Facility Use Request Form
Building Procedures
Key and Alarm Agreements

FAMILY MINISTRY DOCUMENTS

Volunteer Application
Background Check
Curriculum Summary
Oak Leaf Kids Policies and Procedures
Oak Leaf Kids Handbook for Parents
Baby Dedication Philosophy and Information
Fuel Policies and Procedures
Pro-kids Policy

CONNECTIONS DOCUMENTS

Counseling Confidentiality Agreement
Counseling Procedures
First Time Guest Follow Up Process
First Time Guest Form Email
First Time Guest Form Letter
Greeter Handbook
Parking Handbook
Security Plan
List of Counselors for Referral
Journey Group Handbook
New Christian process

New Christian Letter
Baptism Process
Partnership Class Material

Creative Arts Documents

Series Video/Graphic Checklist
Series Planning Timetable
Master Production Checklist
Worship Philosophy
Creative Arts Ministry Manual
Style Guide
Guide to the Giving Talk
Guide to the Welcome
Production Meeting Agenda
Worship Leader Expectations

Financial Documents

Chart of Accounts
Spending Procedures
Offering Count Directions
Benevolence Policy
Finance Team Job Description
Personal Financial Tools
Blank Purchase Requisition
Budget
Budgeting Process
Reimbursement Form

Personnel Documents

Employee Handbook
Blank Housing Allowance Form
Confidentiality Agreement
Employee Handbook Agreement
Employment Application
First Day Checklist for New Hires
Leadership Development Plan
Hiring Process
Interview Questions
New Employee Agreement/Contract
Termination Agreement
Resignation Agreement
6-Month Evaluation
360 Leadership Survey
Staff Job Descriptions
Six-by-Six